OSPREY
PUBLISHING

The Walls of Constantinople AD 324–1453

Stephen Turnbull · Illustrated by Peter Dennis

Series editors Marcus Cowper and Nikolai Bogdanovic

First published in Great Britain in 2004 by Osprey Publishing, Elms Court, Chapel Way, Botley, Oxford OX2 9LP, United Kingdom.
Email: info@ospreypublishing.com

ISBN 1 84176 759 X

SERIES EDITORS: Marcus Cowper and Nikolai Bogdanovic

Editor: Ilios Publishing, Oxford, UK (www.iliospublishing.com)
Design: Ken Vail Graphic Design, Cambridge, UK
Index by David Worthington
Maps by The Map Studio Ltd
Originated by Grasmere Digital Imaging, Leeds, UK
Printed and bound by L-Rex Printing Company Ltd.

04 05 06 07 08   10 9 8 7 6 5 4 3 2 1

A CIP catalogue record for this book is available from the British Library.

FOR A CATALOGUE OF ALL BOOKS PUBLISHED BY OSPREY MILITARY AND AVIATION PLEASE CONTACT:

Osprey Direct USA, c/o MBI Publishing, PO Box 1,
729 Prospect Ave, Osceola, WI 54020, USA.
Email: info@ospreydirectusa.com
Osprey Direct UK, PO Box 140, Wellingborough,
Northants, NN8 2FA, United Kingdom.
Email: info@ospreydirect.co.uk
www.ospreypublishing.com

The Fortress Study Group (FSG)

The object of the FSG is to advance the education of the public in the study of all aspects of fortifications and their armaments, especially works constructed to mount or resist artillery. The FSG holds an annual conference in September over a long weekend with visits and evening lectures, an annual tour abroad lasting about eight days, and an annual Members' Day.

The FSG journal FORT is published annually, and its newsletter Casemate is published three times a year. Membership is international. For further details, please contact:

The Secretary, c/o 6 Lanark Place, London W9 1BS, UK

Author's dedication

To Eileen Brayshaw

Author's acknowledgements

I would first like to thank the staff of certain valuable academic institutions who allowed me access to important source materials. These include in particular the Topkapi Palace Museum and the Military Museum in Istanbul; Cambridge University Library; the Warburg Institute of the University of London; Leeds University Library and Department of Theology and Religious Studies; and the Royal Armouries, Leeds.
No book like this can be written without visiting the site, and my fieldwork for this work actually spans 34 years. In August 1969, as a backpacking student, I made my first visit to Istanbul and had my initial view of the walls of Constantinople from the windows of the Orient Express! I returned in 1996 with my wife and daughter. On this occasion we were accompanied on a walk along the southern section of the walls by four students, two British and two South African, who were teaching English in Istanbul and kindly acted as guides to my wife and me. I revisited Istanbul in June 2003 with my son Richard, whose cheerful and optimistic company allowed me to complete the full circuit of the magnificent walls of Constantinople by foot and by car. This trip with Richard gave me the necessary inspiration to return to the original manuscript of this book, neglected since my wife's death, so I owe him a great debt of gratitude. Finally, I note specially the thoughtfulness shown by Eileen Brayshaw, who took photographs for me of the skyline of Istanbul during her visit, and whose continued support and encouragement then ensured this book was completed.

Artist's note

Readers may care to note that the original paintings from which the colour plates in this book were prepared are available for private sale. The Publishers retain all reproduction copyright whatsoever. All enquiries should be addressed to:

Peter Dennis, The Park, Mansfield, Notts, NG18 2AT

The Publishers regret that they can enter into no correspondence upon this matter.

Editor's note

Unless otherwise indicated, all the images in this book are the property of the author.

Glossary

dromon	A large fast-moving Byzantine galley
mesoteichion	The lowest area of the walls that span the Lycus valley
onager	Catapult where the arm moved through the vertical plne
parateichion	The terrace between the outer wall and the moat
peribolos	The terrace between the inner wall and the outer wall
theotokos	The favoured Byzantine term for the Virgin Mary, literally 'God bearer'

Contents

Introduction

The founding of Constantinople

Constantinople, now Istanbul, takes its name from the Roman emperor Constantine the Great. In the year AD 324 he moved the capital of the Roman Empire eastwards to this site, then called Byzantium, where Europe gazed over into Asia.

Few cities have a more dramatic topography than Constantinople. The new capital was built on a promontory that projects out into the waters of the southern end of the Bosphorus, the narrow strait that connects the Sea of Marmara to the Black Sea. To the south of the promontory the Sea of Marmara spreads out around it like a lake. Beyond this sea to the west lie the straits known as the Dardenelles that give access to the Aegean and the Mediterranean. To the immediate north of the old city is a narrow bay called the Golden Horn. It is one of the finest natural harbours in the world and runs inland for almost seven miles. This was one of Constantinople's most priceless assets.

From ancient times the Bosphorus has been conventionally regarded as separating Europe from Asia. The dramatic and picturesque location of Constantinople on its western shores has therefore ensured that the city should acquire a tremendous symbolic value, giving the site the inevitable romantic associations that have arisen from its position as the 'bridge between east and west' or 'the crossroads of the universe'. It has been such a powerful concept that the image has tended to obscure any serious discussion of the strategic and military considerations that led to Byzantium being chosen as the new capital in the first place. As a result the good points of the strategic and topographical conditions have been exaggerated and the negative points diminished to paint a picture of Constantinople as the ultimate example of perfection attained in the natural strategic defence of a city.

It is therefore somewhat surprising to note that the site of Constantinople was not always so favourably regarded. Byzantium had already existed for 1,000 years before Emperor Constantine came onto the scene, and for most of that time the apparent strategic advantages that we take for granted nowadays were either unrecognised or regarded as irrelevant. For example, the historian Polybius, who lived in the 2nd century BC, wrote that the site of Byzantium may have been favoured for security and prosperity by the sea, 'but as regards the land it is most disadvantageous in both aspects'. In this statement Polybius anticipated why Constantinople's mighty walls should be built in the first

The view of Constantinople as seen from a ship approaching the city from the Sea of Marmara. Of the surviving monuments from Byzantine times, the church of *Haghia Sophia* (Holy Wisdom) appears in the middle distance, with the dome of *Haghia Eirene* (Holy Peace) just visible to its right. This was the glorious city that the walls were built to defend. The sprawl that is modern Istanbul lies in the background. (Photograph by Eileen Brayshaw)

place. Byzantium only looked really formidable when viewed from the seaward side. From the landward side, the future location of the great walls with which this book is concerned, the site looked very vulnerable indeed.

Vulnerable or not, the settlement of Byzantium on the promontory made the location into a position of considerable economic importance. It served naturally and inevitably as a gateway for trade in and out of the Black Sea, but for much of Constantinople's history this factor was far less important than the trade routes coming up from the south. The most important of these was the vital sea traffic that brought food. The Egyptian corn that fed the population until the 7th century AD not only had to travel a distance of 1,000 miles but had to be taken up the Dardanelles at a time when the prevailing winds were northerly.

Polybius's worries about the city's weak defensive points were specifically concerned with the western approach to Constantinople over the flatlands of Thrace that now constitute north-west Turkey. The only mountain ranges in that region run from east to west, and thus afford no natural protection against an invading army. There were also weaknesses to the north because there was no other natural harbour nearby on the Bosphorus, and there was also a long-running problem over water supply to the city. This is a matter that will be discussed in detail later.

The solution to the problem of security from the west is the major theme of this book, because it was for that very reason that the walls of Constantinople were raised. Impregnable by nature to north, east and south, the city had to be made equally impregnable to the west by the hand of man. The results stand today as the greatest surviving monument of military architecture to arise out of the Ancient World and the Middle Ages. Repaired and extended over centuries, the walls of Constantinople withstood sieges delivered by different armies with different weapons and techniques for over a millennium. They stand today partly in romantic ruin, partly as restorations, but everywhere as a splendid testimonial to the men who built them and defended them.

The first fortifications of Constantinople

When Constantine the Great, an experienced soldier, made his momentous decision to turn Byzantium into his capital, his first thoughts naturally turned towards its defence. So, in the year AD 328 the emperor himself traced the limits of the future capital on foot and with his spear in his hand. Some defensive walls had existed from ancient times, but Constantine immediately arranged for new walls to be built. These included an important land wall from the Golden Horn to the Sea of Marmara. The limits that his new walls now enclosed trebled the area formerly occupied by the old Greek city.

The rebuilding of the city as the new imperial capital inevitably encouraged a substantial growth in population. One happy result of this was that when the invading Goths appeared before Constantine's wall in AD 378, following their victory at the battle of Adrianople, they were dissuaded from attacking the city because of the evidence of such a large multitude to oppose them. But the growing population could not forever be housed conveniently within the confines of Constantine's original city plan. Such was the demand for building plots for housing alone that areas of land were reclaimed from the sea. On a larger scale Emperor Valens, for example, erected the fine aqueduct that bears his name in the 4th century AD. This was an enormous project, the scale of which can be gauged from the fact that when it was repaired during the 9th century AD 6,000 labourers had to be brought in for the purpose.

By the time of the reign of Emperor Theodosius II (AD 408–450) the city was threatening to burst the confines that Constantine had erected. Something had to be done, but by the first half of the 5th century AD the population explosion in Constantinople was not the most important consideration occupying imperial minds. Rome, the former capital of the Empire, had been captured by

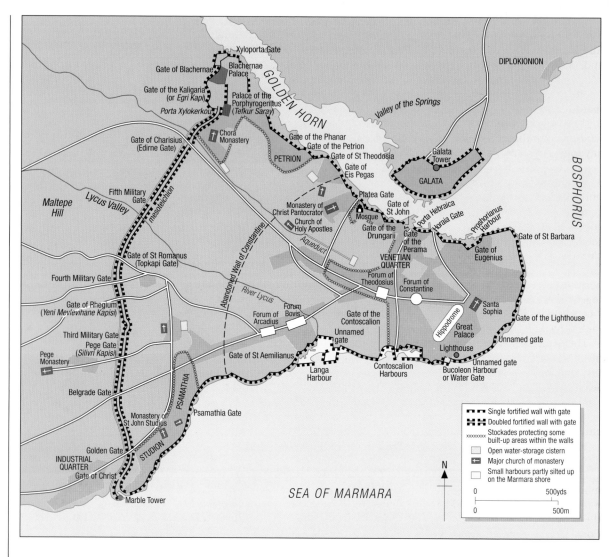

Single fortified wall with gate
Doubled fortified wall with gate
Stockades protecting some built-up areas within the walls
Open water-storage cistern
Major church of monastery
Small harbours partly silted up on the Marmara shore

Map of Constantinople showing the line of the Theodosian walls and the sea walls. The course of the walls of Constantine the Great is shown as a dotted line. (© Copyright Osprey Publishing Limited)

the Goths. The Huns had also crossed the Danube, and although they had been driven back there was a real fear that they would return to pose a direct threat to Constantinople.

It was therefore most fortunate for the Byzantine Empire that when the hour came, along too came the man. His name was Anthemius, and he headed the Byzantine government during the minority of Emperor Theodosius II. From the time of his appointment as Praetorian Prefect of the East in AD 405, Anthemius applied himself with vigour to whatever task the empire demanded of him. The first task was the expulsion of the Huns from the Balkans. The second resulted in the walls of Constantinople.

The so-called Theodosian walls (nothing so grand could bear the name of anyone less than the ruling emperor) were the results of Anthemius' skilled and dedicated work. His walls set in stone the limits that Constantinople was to possess and to defend until modern times. Today's tourists to Istanbul find Anthemius' limits marked on the map as the 'Old City': an apparently tiny element in the modern sprawl that now stretches far up the Bosphorus past the two recently built suspension bridges. But that sprawl is modern Istanbul. The Theodosian walls defined what for the next 1,500 years was to be understood as Constantinople.

The Theodosian walls

The Theodosian walls were built about 1½ miles west of Constantine's original fortifications. The area occupied by the city was therefore greatly increased, and, most suitably for the city that had inherited the mantle of Rome, the completed Theodosian walls of Constantinople enclosed seven hills.

From the moment that Anthemius' designs began to take shape the erection, maintenance and repair of the new fortifications of the city became an undertaking in which all citizens were required to assist in one form or another. On that point the laws were very strict, and neither rank nor privilege exempted anyone from their obligation to carry out the work. One-third of the annual land tax of the city went towards the cost of the walls, and any additional expenditure was provided by requisitions laid upon the inhabitants. There does not seem to have been much grumbling about the matter. Indeed, there was a genuine enthusiasm for a project that promised increased security, and the government harnessed such enthusiasm in various ways. One subtle ploy was the way the government appealed to the citizens' generosity according to which circus faction they belonged to. These factions, among them the Blues and the Greens, were the supporters of chariot-racing teams. They were great rivals when cheering on their side from the terraces of the Hippodrome, but worked together on the walls when the city was threatened. Records show that in AD 447, when repairs were being undertaken, the Blues and Greens supplied 16,000 men between them for the building effort.

The walls designed by Anthemius were completed in the year AD 423, the fifth year of the reign of Theodosius II, who was then about 12 years old. They survive today as the inner wall of the fortification line that extends from the Sea of Marmara to the ruins of the Byzantine Palace of the Porphyrogenitus (*Tekfur Saray*). The increase in the area they enclosed also necessitated an extension of the sea walls along the northern and southern shores of the city, although these works were not carried out until some time later.

The first challenge faced by the original line of the Theodosian walls was provided by nature. In AD 447, only 34 years after their construction, the greater part of the new walls, including 57 towers, was flattened by a series of mighty earthquakes. The timing could not have been worse as Attila the Hun was advancing on Constantinople. Fortunately, in a splendid confirmation of the energy and commitment to their defence that the citizens of Constantinople had shown before, the government and people rose to the challenge and restored the fallen walls in less than three months. These new walls helped to save Constantinople from Attila, although other sources tell of an epidemic among his followers.

Strangely enough, we do not know for certain the name of the man who took the lead in this great endeavour. He may have been called Constantine or

A very damaged octagonal tower from the inner section of the Theodosian walls, located just to the south of the Golden Gate.

Cyrus, and he was the then Praetorian Prefect of the East. Our anonymous hero went much further than mere restoration, and took the opportunity to make the city into a much stronger fortress than even Anthemius had dared to contemplate. An extra wall was built outside Anthemius' wall, with a broad and deep moat in front of it. When the work was complete the city lay behind three lines of defence and 192 towers flanked the walls. It was these walls that were to prove impregnable for the next 1,000 years and survive to this day.

The later walls

Although the Theodosian walls described above constitute the greater part of what is now visible on the ground, even the most cursory visitor cannot help but notice that towards the northern extremity of the walls there is a change in design. Just before they head downhill towards the Golden Horn, the Theodosian walls come to an abrupt end and are replaced by a wall of more complex and different construction. This is something of a puzzle. Surely the Theodosian walls originally extended all the way to the Golden Horn, so why were they replaced?

The explanation begins in AD 627 during the reign of Emperor Heraclius, when the quarter called Blachernae was actually a suburb outside the line of the Theodosian walls. It contained a church called the Church of the *Theotokos*, or Mother of God, and it was believed that the holiness of the site and the relic it contained would protect it from danger. But in AD 627 Constantinople was attacked by the Avars, who devastated the area around. Even though the church suffered no harm it prompted the realisation that a wall should enclose it for extra security. Blachernae therefore received the protection of a wall, and further additions were made in AD 813 under Emperor Leo the Armenian in the face of threats from the Bulgarians.

The Blachernae area grew in importance over the next few centuries. It even acquired one of Constantinople's most important buildings. This was the imperial palace of Blachernae, which became the favourite residence of the imperial court during the reign of Alexius I Comnenus (AD 1081–1118). It was a peaceful spot away from the hustle and bustle of the city, but its remoteness made it a prime target for any attack, so there was a constant need to review the defences in this quarter and, if necessary, enhance them. Additions were therefore made, and the walls that now surround the Blachernae Palace area are the walls built during the reign of Emperor Manuel Comnenus (AD 1143–80). According to the historian Nicetas Choniates, the camp pitched by the armies of the Fourth Crusade in 1203 lay 'on a hill overlooking the wall built by Emperor Manuel'. These were the final pieces of the jigsaw that now make up the walls of Constantinople.

To the left lies the restored section around the Belgrade Gate, typical of the stronger of the entrances to the city.

Chronology

The point where the Theodosian walls give way to the Comnenan walls near the Palace of the Porphyrogenitus. The change in style is quite striking. Several centuries separate the two constructions.

Design and development

The material structure of the walls

A cross-section of the Theodosian walls of Anthemius reveals three layers of defence. From the city side outwards, there is first the inner wall. A narrow walkway divides this from the outer wall, which is both lower and weaker. A wider outer walkway ends with another low wall that is the inner side of the moat. On the other side of the moat the ground is flat.

The standard building materials of Constantinople were squared stone, brick and lime mortar. To these could be added marble, sometimes in the form of reused pieces taken from older sites. The region around the Sea of Marmara offered a rich variety of natural stones, for which there were numerous quarries. The stone sections in the walls were built from tertiary limestone brought from the quarries located about three miles to the west of the Golden Gate.

Bricks must have been produced locally, although no remains of Byzantine kilns have been found. Mortar was made by mixing lime with various aggregates, often brick dust and fragments. Byzantine mortar was particularly strong once it had hardened. The other building material seen in some places on the wall would have been roof tiles used for decoration, for example to make an arch-shape to frame an inscription.

The foundations of Byzantine churches were constructed of brick or stone, and if possible cut to the bedrock, so the city walls were probably underpinned in a similar way. Byzantine walls were generally constructed of alternating bands of brick and stone. Squared stone faced both the inner and outer surfaces of the wall, and mortared rubble filled the space in between the facings. The Theodosian walls were no exception to this general pattern. The bricks normally formed a levelling course, extending through the thickness of the walls and binding the two faces together, so that when a brick course appears on the outside of a wall, we should expect to see the same course on the inner.

In the inner wall six brick courses, each containing five layers of bricks, were laid at intervals through the thickness of the walls to bind the structure more

The Theodosian walls were constructed using stone and brick. In this detail of the sea wall on the Sea of Marmara both materials can be seen. Brick was used more sparingly than stone.

Cross-section and plan of the Theodosian walls

This plate shows a complete cross-section and plan of a typical stretch of the Theodosian walls. The section shows the different layers of defence. On the plan are the different shapes of towers.

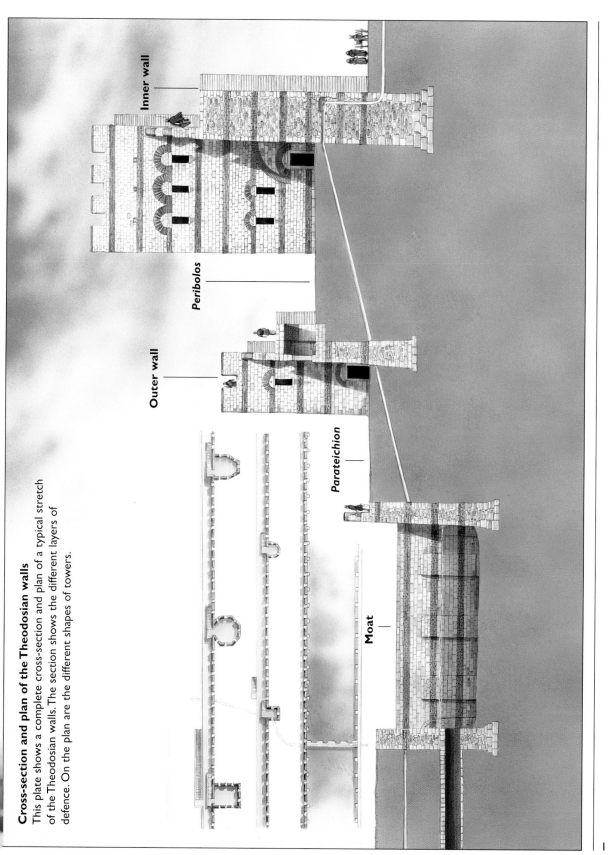

Inner wall

Peribolos

Outer wall

Parateichion

Moat

firmly. The bricks used are from 1ft in. to 1ft 2in. square and 2in. thick. They are sometimes stamped with the name of their manufacturer or donor, and occasionally bear the name of the contemporary emperor and some indication of where they were made.

The inner wall

The strongest part of the wall along its entire length was the inner wall. This magnificent structure, nearly all of which is still visible either as ruins or modern reconstruction, stood on a higher level than the outer wall and was loftier, thicker and flanked by stronger towers. The inner wall rises some 30ft 6in. above the present exterior ground level and about 40ft above the level within the city, with a thickness varying from 15ft 6in. near the base to 13ft 6in. at the top. There was a battlemented row along the outer edge 4ft 8in. high. This was the main defensive platform, and was reached by flights of stone steps set at right angles to the wall above ramps of masonry.

The inner wall originally sported no less than 96 towers. They were spaced between 175 and 181ft apart and were from 57 to 60ft high with a projection of 18 to 34ft. Their shape is interesting, because while most are of square cross-section some are hexagonal, while others are heptagonal or octagonal. Although lying along the wall, the towers were part of the same construction, but were built as separate structures. This ensured that different rates of settlement would not cause them to break apart.

Wooden or vaulted floors usually divided each tower into two chambers. The lower chamber was entered from the city by a large archway. This entrance provided most of the light and air for the room, because defensive considerations did not permit large windows. This chamber had little to do with the defence of the city but served as a storeroom or guardhouse. In some cases a narrow postern gate in the angle of the wall allowed access to the walkway between the two sets of walls. Further security considerations also meant that, as a general rule, the lower room had no means of communication with the room above. This was instead entered only from the battlement level by an arched doorway. The upper room was well lit by comparatively large windows that allowed the defenders a good field of view and also permitted them to fire freely upon attackers. A flight of stairs allowed access to the third

Towers and walls of the inner wall between the Golden Gate and the Belgrade Gate. The first tower is octagonal. Although damaged here, we can also clearly see the outer wall, the other small wall outside the outer walk and the moat, here flooded.

and uppermost defensive level of the tower. This was the battlemented roof. In times of siege catapults, and later cannon, could be mounted.

The outer wall

The terrace between the inner and outer walls was called the *peribolos*, and accommodated the soldiers who defended the outer wall. It was between 50 and 64ft wide. Beyond lay the outer wall, which was a modest structure compared to the inner wall. It was nonetheless a vital line of defence, and during the fierce sieges of AD 1422 and 1453 the most desperate fighting occurred here.

The outer wall is from 2ft to 6ft 6in. thick, rising some 10ft above the present level of the *peribolos* and about 27ft 6in. above the present level of the terrace between the outer wall and the moat. Its lower portion is a solid wall that retains the embankment of the *peribolos*. The upper portion is built for the most part in arches, faced on the outer side with hewn blocks of stone, and is frequently supported by a series of such arches in concrete. The arches strengthened the wall and allowed the construction of a battlement and parapet walk on the upper surface. The arches also formed chambers 8ft 6in. deep where soldiers could be safely sheltered and accommodated.

The towers in the outer wall are much smaller than those in the inner wall. They are some 30 to 35ft high, projecting about 16ft beyond the curtain wall, and are spaced out so as to alternate with the towers of the inner wall. They appear to have been designed in alternate shapes of squares and crescents, although later repairs have spoiled the pattern. Each tower had a chamber on the level of the *peribolos* that was provided with small windows. The lower portion of most of the towers was generally a solid substructure, but in the case of the square towers it was often a small chamber reached from the outer terrace by a small postern gate and leading to a subterranean passage running towards the city.

The outer terrace and moat

The terrace between the outer wall and the moat is about 61ft wide. It was known as the *parateichion*, and its main function was to extend the distance between the besiegers and the besieged.

The moat is over 61ft wide and over 20ft deep. On its inner and outer sides (in military terminology the scarp and counterscarp) there is masonry 5ft thick, and buttresses support it. The small defensive wall on the scarp is about 6ft 6in. high. Across the moat are found long low walls that appear to divide the moat into several compartments. These contain hidden aqueducts for the supply of water to the city.

The gates of the city

The Theodosian walls were pierced by ten main gates and several small postern gates. Postern gates were few in number for security reasons and almost all were

ABOVE TOP Looking from inside the city we see a military gate, a walkway, an outer staircase and the arches of the inner wall in a section near the Edirne Gate.

ABOVE BOTTOM The *peribolos*, the area between the inner and outer walls, looking north from the Belgrade Gate. Some of the fiercest fighting during the AD 1453 siege occurred in this area between the two defences.

Walkway

Inner wall

Entrance to city

A tower in the Theodosian walls c. AD 447
A cutaway section of one of the towers of the Theodosian walls, showing how the two levels of the towers were entirely separate. The lower room was entered from the city, the upper from the battlemented walkway.

located in the inner wall. The main gates can be divided into two types: the military gates that led to different parts of the fortifications and the public gates that were the entrances to the city by means of bridges across the moat. The two series followed each other in alternate order, the military entrances being known by numbers and the public gates by proper names. Both the public and the military gates shared a common overall design. All were double gateways because they had to pierce two walls. The inner gateway, being the principal one, was built into the inner wall of the Theodosian line. Two large towers that projected far beyond the curtain wall guarded all the gateways. The towers were of very similar design to the towers found along the length of the walls as described above. The Belgrade Gate provides an excellent example of this, showing how the projecting walls would allow defenders to achieve good flanking fire and to protect the outer gateway by archery. The other intention behind the design was that the distance across the *peribolos* between the two sets of gates should be made deliberately as narrow as possible. By contrast, the gates in the outer walls were quite modest affairs, consisting of a simple gated arch not much higher than the outer wall level.

ABOVE LEFT A tower in the *mesoteichion*. The two floors were totally separate inside.

ABOVE RIGHT A restored tower near the Edirne Gate, showing the use of stone and brick. Brick appears as arches above windows and in thin layers. The author is shown for comparison with the size of the building. (Photograph by Richard Turnbull)

The sea walls

As the line of the land walls expanded outwards under Constantine I and Thedosius II so the sea walls grew to meet them. They are of similar construction to the land walls, but nowhere were they as formidable, and nowadays they exist only as short stretches of fragments, though some have been restored.

The sea walls of Constantinople were always less spectacular in appearance than the land walls, and were to some extent less important in the city's defence. As long as the emperor retained control of the sea, a city accessible only by water through the narrow defiles of the Dardanelles and the Bosphorus had

The battlemented walkway of the inner wall looking south from the Belgrade Gate into the city.

little to fear from a naval attack. This immunity was compromised when the Ottomans and the Italian republics became maritime powers. But even then the position of the city rendered a seaborne attack a difficult proposition. The northern shore of the city could be put beyond the reach of an enemy by stretching a chain across the narrow entrance to the Golden Horn, while the currents in the Sea of Marmara could always carry an attacking fleet out to sea or fling it against rocks. According to Villehardouin, it was the fear of these currents that dissuaded Dandolo's crusaders from attacking along the coastline of the Sea of Marmara.

The chain on the Golden Horn passed between two towers and was supported in the water by wooden floats. It is first mentioned in connection with the siege of AD 717–18 when Emperor Leo lowered the chain in the hope of enticing the enemy fleet into the harbour. It was also used by Nicephorus Phocas against an expected Russian attack during the AD 960s, but in AD 1203 the crusading army simply removed it once they had captured the northern anchor point to which it was secured. It managed to frustrate Mehmet the Conqueror in AD 1453, who as a result was driven to the ingenious and successful method of dragging his ships overland. In the long history of the Byzantine Empire there was only one instance of a successful naval assault on Constantinople. This was the capture of the city in AD 1204 by the Venetian crusaders after they had destroyed the chain's anchor tower.

The need for sea defences also provided some concern in AD 1351 when a powerful Genoese fleet sailed to attack Constantinople in support of certain claims put forth by the Genoese colony at Galata. On its way through the Sea of Marmara the Genoese fleet captured the fortified town of Heraclea. This event caused great consternation in the capital, and in view of the enemy's approach the reigning emperor promptly put the sea walls in order, repairing them where they were ruined, raising their height and ordering all houses in front of them to be removed. He also increased the height of the towers.

Repairing and maintaining the walls

The walls of Constantinople had to be kept in a good state of repair, so designated officers, known variously as Governors of the Walls or Counts of the Walls, had the job of taking charge of repairs and maintenance.

Most of the damage the walls sustained came from the effects of weather or earthquakes, not war. The walls were so strong that little battle damage was sustained until very late in their history when gunpowder was employed. Earthquakes, by contrast, led to the initial rebuilding at the time of Attila the Hun and to damage in AD 542, 554 and 558. The latter disaster occurred during the reign of Justinian, who was so despondent that he refused to wear his crown for the next 30 days. The subsequent rebuilding, however, was thorough enough to allow the great general Belisarius to repel the Huns from the walls when the raiders appeared again in AD 559. Repairs were also undertaken when danger threatened, as happened early in the 8th century AD when a further attack by the Arabs was expected. The most extensive work in the wall's history

after AD 447 was made in AD 1345 when the entire length of the walls was repaired and strengthened in the face of an attack by a rival emperor.

The most important example of the walls being restored after war damage occurred following the 57 years of Latin occupation of the city that resulted from the disaster of the Fourth Crusade in AD 1204. When Emperor Michael VIII Palaeologus made his triumphant entry to the city in AD 1261 he was shocked and dismayed by the ruinous condition of the city and its walls. During the initial siege of AD 1203 catapult stones had rained down on the Blachernae Palace and a battering ram had broken through a section of the walls. There had then been years of looting and neglect. A recent estimate concludes that during the Latin occupation one-sixth of the area of Constantinople was ravaged by fire and between one-sixth and one-third of its buildings destroyed.

The repair of the walls was one of the new emperor's top priorities, because an attempt by the Latin forces to regain control was daily expected. The land walls were in such a bad condition that even when the gates were closed it was easy to get in and out of the city, but at that time there was more concern about the sea walls. The Genoese were now established across the Golden Horn in Galata, and their ships passed defiantly up and down below the sea walls. There was no time to build from stone, so as a temporary measure Michael VIII immediately ordered that the height of the sea walls be increased by about 7ft by the addition of wooden screens, which were covered in leather hide to make them fire proof. Later in his reign Michael VIII is believed to have had a second line of sea walls built so that they matched the fortifications of the land walls. However, the new line cannot have been very substantial because no trace of them has survived and some authorities doubt if they were ever built at all.

A section of sea wall on the Sea of Marmara. The sea walls compare in strength to the outer walls of the Theodosian land walls.

RIGHT The chain that was slung across the Golden Horn during sieges is preserved here in the Military Museum in Istanbul. Each link is about 2ft long. It was only broken once in a siege, that occasion being the capture of Constantinople during the Fourth Crusade in AD 1204.

BELOW The view looking along the very damaged section of wall north of the Golden Gate towards the Belgrade Gate.

Like the Theodosian walls, the later sections around the Blachernae Palace were repaired time and again, and several inscriptions testify to this. For example, in AD 1317 Empress Irene, the consort of Andronicus II, died and left a large sum of money that the emperor devoted to the restoration of the walls. A later inscription mentions repairs undertaken by John VII Palaeologus in AD 1441, just over a decade before the fall of Constantinople to the Ottomans. The outer wall received the major attention on this occasion.

Tour of the site

BELOW TOP The southern tip of the walls at the Sea of Marmara, looking from the Golden Gate towards the sea.

BELOW BOTTOM The Marble Tower stands on a little promontory by the sea. Its lower half is faced with marble, and is unlike any other structure along the entire length. It is likely that the Marble Tower did not primarily form part of the defensive structure, but was instead an imperial sea pavilion.

From the Marble Tower to the Golden Gate

The best way of understanding the layout of the walls of Constantinople and the succession of construction phases is to take a hypothetical tour from one end to the other. We will begin at the southern extremity where the Theodosian walls reach the Sea of Marmara. Heading north we will pass the Golden Gate and the Yedikule fortress, taking in the major stretches of the best preserved wall. We will then descend into the Lycus Valley, rising up again to the Palace of the Porphyrogenitus. The line of walls that follows are the later ones that take us down to the Golden Horn.

As noted above, the walls of Constantinople enclose an area running from the Sea of Marmara in the south to the natural harbour of the Golden Horn to the north. They are anchored at their southern extremity by the so-called Marble Tower. This handsome structure stands on a little promontory by the sea. Its lower half is faced with marble, and is unlike any other structure along the entire length. It is likely that the Marble Tower did not primarily form part of the defensive structure, but was instead an imperial sea pavilion, a sort of fortified villa for the imperial party. The tower also served for some time as a prison, and one can still see the chute down which the bodies of the executed were thrown into the sea.

The first tower of the Theodosian walls lies just to the north of the Marble Tower. It is in a fine state of preservation, as is the first of the ancient gateways to the city. This is the Gate of Christ, so-called because of the monogram 'XP' above it. The Gate of Christ was also known as the First Military Gate. Just to the north the railway cuts through the circuit of the walls between the seventh and eighth towers of the inner wall. The eighth tower of the inner wall forms the south-western corner of Yedikule, the Ottoman 'castle of the seven towers' described below, while the ninth and tenth towers are the two marble towers flanking the famous Golden Gate. These towers are also part of Yedikule, as is the eleventh and last tower in this first stretch of the Theodosian Walls. Immediately beyond this last tower is *Yedikule Kapisi*, the modern name of a small portal that was the public entrance into this part of the city in Byzantine times. In the interior above the arch of this gate there is the figure of an imperial Byzantine eagle represented in white marble.

The Golden Gate

From the point of view of this book the most interesting part of the Yedikule complex is the Golden Gate. Although it was completely integrated into the defensive system many centuries ago it is actually a Roman triumphal arch erected in about AD 390 by Theodosius I, known as the Great. At that time the city walls had not been built and the triumphal arch, as was customary, stood by itself on the road called the *Via Egnatia*. The arch was of the usual Roman form, with a triple arcade consisting of a large central archway flanked by two smaller ones. The outlines of the arches can still be seen clearly although the openings were bricked up in later Byzantine times. The name *Porta Aurea* (Golden Gate) probably comes from gold decorations on the arches. Travellers described them as 'glittering with gold'.

The facade was decorated with sculptures, the most famous of which was a group of four elephants placed there to commemorate the triumphal entry of

The octagonal tower just to the south of the Golden Gate, which is visible in the distance. The use of alternate layers of brick and stone is well shown.

The twin towers outside the Golden Gate, the means whereby this originally triumphal arch became integrated into the defensive system.

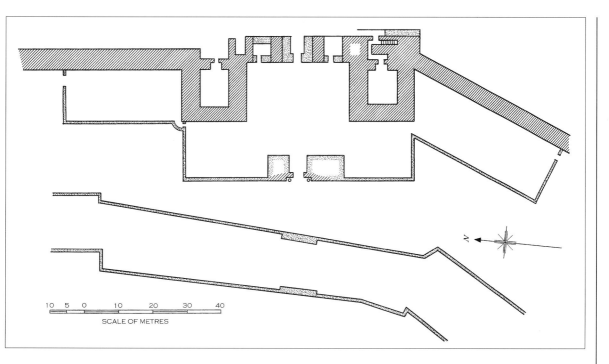

SCALE OF METRES

Theodosius the Great after his victory over Maxentius. When Theodosius II decided to extend the city walls two decades later he incorporated the Golden Gate within his new land walls. It was presumably in connection with this new wall that he built the small marble gate outside the triumphal arch. The arch itself would have had no gates, except for ornamental iron or bronze grilles, and would have been indefensible. The outer gateway thus became part of the general system of defence and, together with the curtain walls that join it to the city walls near the polygonal towers, forms a small courtyard in front of the Golden Gate.

On many occasions after the time of Theodosius the Great the Golden Gate became the scene of triumphal entries by Byzantine emperors: Heraclius in AD 629 after he saved the empire by defeating the Persians; Constantine V, Basil I, and Basil II after their victories over the Bulgars; John I Tzimisces after his defeat of the Russians; and Theophilus and his son Michael III after their victories over the Arabs. Perhaps the most emotional of all these triumphal entries was that of 15 August 1261, when Michael VIII Palaeologus rode in triumph and gratitude through the Golden Gate on a white charger after Constantinople was recaptured from the Latins who had taken it during the Fourth Crusade of AD 1204. This was the last time an emperor of Byzantium rode in triumph through the Golden Gate. In its last two centuries the history of the empire was one of continuing defeat, and by that time the Golden Gate had been walled up for defence, never again to open.

From the Golden Gate to *Silivri Kapisi* (the Gate of the Spring)

From the Golden Gate to the next gate, *Belgrad Kapisi* (the Belgrade Gate), it is possible to walk either on top of the great wall or on the terrace below, for the fortifications along this stretch are in quite good condition. All of the 11 towers that guard the wall along this line are still standing, as are all but one of those in the outer wall. An inscription on the eighth tower of the inner wall records repairs by Leo III and Constantine V in the years AD 720 to 741, and one on the tenth tower of the outer wall states that John VIII Palaeologus restored it in AD 1434.

A plan of the Golden Gate showing how the defensive walls were built around it. (© Copyright Osprey Publishing Limited, artwork by John Richards)

RIGHT The Golden Gate was originally a Roman triumphal arch. It was walled up for defence during the last two centuries of the Byzantine Empire. The author's wife standing outside shows how large the entrance was.

BELOW This is the Gate of Christ, so-called because of the monogram 'XP' above it. The Gate of Christ was also known as the First Military Gate.

The Belgrade Gate was known in Byzantine times as the Second Military Gate. It was also called *Porta tou Deuterou*, because it led to the military quarter of Deuteros, where the Gothic soldiers had their barracks during the early Byzantine period. This was the largest of all the military gates and may also have been used by the general public, as indeed it has been ever since. The gate came by its Turkish name because Suleiman the Magnificent settled in its vicinity many of the artisans he brought back with him from Belgrade after his capture of that city in AD 1521.

The stretch of walls from *Belgrad Kapisi* to the next town gate, *Silivri Kapisi*, is also in good condition, with all 13 towers still standing in the inner wall and only one missing in the outer. The third and fourth towers of the inner walls both bear inscriptions of Leo III and Constantine V; while the fifth, tenth, and twelfth towers have inscriptions of John VIII, the first dated AD 1440 and the second and third AD 1434.

Silivri Kapisi was known in Byzantium as the Pege Gate, or the Gate of the Spring, because it was near the celebrated shrine of Zoodochus Pege. Like all of the larger gates, it is a double gate with entrances through both the inner and outer walls. On the southern tower beside the gate there is an inscription dated AD 1438 and recording a repair by Manuel Bryennius, a nobleman in the reign of John VIII, and on the north tower there is an inscription of

The Golden Gate c. AD 850

This plate shows the Golden Gate as it would have appeared during the reign of Emperor Michael III (AD 842–867). The Golden Gate is actually a Roman triumphal arch erected in about AD 390. When Theodosius II decided to extend the city walls two decades later he incorporated the Golden Gate within his new land walls. We see the gate here in its dual role of fortification and major entrance to the city. The sculptures that adorn it are ones that are known to have existed at the time of Michael III and consist of two Winged Victories, female figures representing the fortune of the city and, four bronze elephants.

HAEC LOCA THEVDOSIVS DECORAT POST FATA TYRANNI. AVREA SAECLA GERIT QVI PORTAM CONSTRVIT AVRO.

23

ABOVE A view looking up to the outer and inner walls from the area just north of the Golden Gate. The towers of the Yedikule fortress can be seen just behind the line of the inner wall.

RIGHT The Belgrade Gate was known in Byzantine times as the Second Military Gate. It was where the Gothic soldiers had their barracks during the early Byzantine period. This was the largest of all the military gates and the public may also have used it, as indeed they have ever since.

Basil II (AD 976–1025) and his brother Constantine VIII (AD 1025–28). The most memorable day in the history of this gate was 25 July 1261. On that day a small body of Byzantine troops led by Alexius Strategopoulos overpowered the Latin guards at the gate and forced their way inside, thus opening the way to the recapture of Constantinople and the restoration of the Byzantine Empire to its ancient capital.

From *Silivri Kapisi* (the Gate of the Spring) to *Yeni Mevlevihane Kapisi* (the Gate of Rhegium)

All of the original 15 towers are still standing in the stretch of wall between the two gates of *Silivri Kapisi* and *Yeni Mevlevihane Kapisi*, but neither they nor the walls themselves are as well preserved as those closer to the Sea of Marmara. Between the fifth and seventh towers there is a curious indentation in the wall.

ABOVE *Silivri Kapisi* was known in Byzantium as the Pege Gate, or the Gate of the Spring, because it was near the celebrated shrine of Zoodochus Pege. Like all of the larger gates, it is a double gate with entrances through both the inner and outer walls.

LEFT The Yeni Mevlevi Gate. *Yeni Mevlevihane Kapisi* takes its modern Turkish name from the headquarters of a group of Mevlevi dervishes that once stood outside the gate. In Byzantium it was called the Gate of Rhegium, and sometimes also the Gate of the Reds after the circus faction that built it.

This is known as the Sigma because its shape resembles the uncial form of that Greek letter, which is like the letter C. Just beyond the Sigma is the Third Military Gate, now walled up. Over this little gate there once stood a statue of Theodosius II, builder of these great walls. The statue did not disappear until the 14th century. The second tower of the inner wall bears an inscription of Leo III and Constantine V, and on the tenth tower is one with the names of Leo IV (AD 775–80), Constantine VI (AD 780–97), and the Empress Irene (AD 797–802).

Yeni Mevlevihane Kapisi takes its modern Turkish name from the headquarters of a group of Mevlevi dervishes that once stood outside the gate. In Byzantium it was called the Gate of Rhegium, and sometimes also the Gate of the Reds after the circus faction that built it. The gateway is remarkable for the number of inscriptions preserved upon it. One inscription mentions the Red faction and is undoubtedly of AD 447, when the final phase of the Theodosian walls was completed by Constantine, Prefect of the East. This great feat is commemorated in two inscriptions on the south corbel of the outer gate, one in Greek and the other in Latin. The Greek inscription merely gives the facts of construction. The Latin one is more boastful, reading, 'By the command of Theodosius, Constantine erected these strong walls in less than two months. Scarcely could Pallas herself have built so strong a citadel in so short a span'. There is also an inscription on the lintel of the outer gate recording a restoration by Justin II (AD 565–78), his wife Sophia, and Narses, the eunuch who succeeded Belisarius as commander of the Byzantine army.

From *Yeni Mevlevihane Kapisi* (the Gate of Rhegium) to *Porta Xylokerkou* (the Gate of the Wooden Circus)

The stretch between these two gates forms the centre of the long arc of walls. The seventh tower of the inner wall bears the names of Leo III and Constantine V, along with this inscription: 'Oh Christ, God, preserve thy city undisturbed and free from war. Conquer the wrath of our enemies'. Between the ninth and tenth towers the Fourth Military Gate, now closed up, pierces the inner wall. On the first tower of the wall north of this gate there is an inscription mentioning a certain Georgius. This is believed to have been removed from a nearby church and placed in the walls during the restoration by John VIII in AD 1438/39, evidence that many buildings near the walls were torn down to strengthen them against the impending siege by the Turks.

The stretch of fortifications between the two gates of Romanus and Charisius (Top Kapi and Edirne respectively) was known in Byzantium as the *mesoteichion*. This part of the walls was the most vulnerable in the whole defence system, because here the fortifications descend very noticeably into the valley of the Lycus, the stream that entered the city midway between the two

Towers of the inner wall and damaged sections of the outer wall shown near the Topkapi Gate where a modern road cuts through the wall.

gates. During the last siege in 1453 the defenders on the *mesoteichion* were at a serious disadvantage because they lay below the level of the Turkish guns on either side of the valley. For that reason the walls in the Lycus Valley are the most badly damaged in the whole length of the fortifications, and most of the defence towers are mere piles of rubble or great shapeless hulks of masonry. The course of the ancient river Lycus is today marked by the broad new road, called *Vatan Caddesi*, which breaches the walls midway between *Top Kapi* and *Edirne Kapisi*. Just inside the walls between this breach and the Fifth Military Gate is the area called *Sulukule*. Since late Byzantine times this has been the Gypsy quarter of the city, and, despite frequent attempts by the authorities to evict them, the Gypsies still live there in ramshackle wooden houses built right up against the Theodosian walls. The section of walls in this area was originally known as the *Murus Bacchatureus*. According to tradition this is where Constantine XI had his command post during the last siege. He was last seen there just before the walls were breached, fighting valiantly.

The Fifth Military Gate is known in Turkish as *Hucum Kapisi* (the Gate of the Assault) to preserve the memory of that last battle. On the outer lintel of the gate there is an inscription recording a repair by one Pusaeus, dated to the 5th century AD. On the eighth tower there is an inscription of John VIII dated AD 1433 and another by one Manuel Iagari in the reign of Constantine XI (AD 1449–53). The latter inscription is the latest record of a repair to the walls, and it was probably placed there at the time of the preparations for the final siege in AD 1453.

The Edirne Gate (the Gate of Charisius) stands at the peak of the sixth hill and is thus at the highest point in the old city, 40ft above sea level. This gate has preserved in Turkish form one of its ancient names, as from here the main

ABOVE LEFT A fragment of wall in the *mesoteichion*. This was the lowest lying section of the Theodosian walls where they crossed the Lycus Valley.

ABOVE RIGHT Artillery damage in the *mesoteichion*. The destruction wrought by Mehmet the Conqueror's artillery and the subsequent ravages of time allow us to see the interior of a tower on the inner wall.

The Edirne Gate (the Gate of Charisius) stands at the peak of the sixth hill and is thus at the highest point in the old city, 40ft above sea level. This gate was originally called the *Porta Adrianopoleos*, as from here the main road went to Adrianople (the modern Edirne).

road went to Adrianople (the modern Edirne). It was also known in Byzantium as the Gate of Charisius, or sometimes as the *Porta Polyandriou*, the Gate of the Cemetery. This latter name came from the large necropolis outside the walls in this area. The graveyard still exists and displays large Turkish, Greek and Armenian burial grounds, the latter two probably dating from Byzantine times.

It was through the Edirne Gate that Mehmet II made his triumphal entry after his capture of Constantinople early in the afternoon of 29 May 1453, and a plaque on the southern side of the gate commemorates that historic event. Just inside the Edirne Gate to the south stands the splendid *Mihrimah Sultan Camii*, one of the great imperial mosques of Constantinople.

The Theodosian walls continue on for about 700 yards beyond *Edirne Kapisi*, at which point they give way to the stretch of walls constructed in later times. The inner wall in this stretch is well preserved and has nine towers that are more or less intact. At the very end of the existing Theodosian walls, just next to its last tower, are the remains of a small postern that played a fateful role in the final hours of the last siege. This is the *Porta Xylokerkou*, the Gate of the Wooden Circus, named after a hippodrome that once stood outside the walls in this area. At the climax of the last battle on 29 May 1453 this gate was left open and unguarded for a few moments, and it was through here that the Janissaries first made their way into the city. It was also from the tower beside the *Porta Xylokerkou*, the very last bastion on the long line of the Theodosian walls, that the Turkish ensign first waved over Constantinople.

The Palace of the Porphyrogenitus (*Tekfur Saray*)

Just beyond this gate there stands one of the most remarkable buildings remaining from the days of Byzantium. It is known in Turkish as *Tekfur Saray*, the Palace of the Sovereign, but it is better known in English as the Palace of

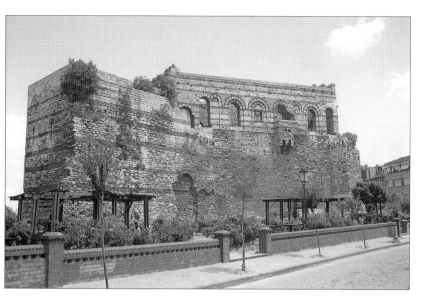

The Palace of the Porphyrogenitus. Just in front of the ruins may be seen the remains of the *Porta Xylokerkou*, the Gate of the Wooden Circus, named after a hippodrome that once stood outside the walls in this area. At the climax of the last battle on 29 May 1453 this gate was left open and unguarded for a few moments, and it was through here that the Janissaries first made their way into the city.

the Porphyrogenitus. The palace was probably built in the latter part of the 13th century or early in the 14th century and served as one of the imperial residences during the last two centuries of Byzantium. It is a large three-storied building wedged in between the inner and outer fortifications of the last stretch of the Theodosian walls. On the ground floor an arcade, with four wide arches, opens on to the courtyard, which is overlooked on the first floor by five large windows. The top floor, which projects above the walls, has windows on all sides, seven overlooking the courtyard, a curious bow-like apse on the opposite side, and a window with the remains of a balcony to the east. The roof and all of the floors have disappeared. The whole palace, but especially the facade on the court, is elaborately decorated with geometrical designs in red brick and white marble.

From the Palace of the Porphyrogenitus (*Tekfur Saray*) to the Golden Horn

Just beyond *Tekfur Saray* the Theodosian walls come to an abrupt end and walls of later construction continue the fortifications. As noted earlier, there has been much discussion about the original course of the Theodosian walls from *Tekfur Saray* down to the Golden Horn. It would appear that they turned almost due north at *Tekfur Saray* and from there followed a more or less straight line down to the Golden Horn, whereas the later walls are bent in an arc farther out to the west. Stretches of what are undoubtedly the original Theodosian walls can be seen at *Tekfur Saray* and also along a nearby street where the ruined walls are quite impressive and picturesque. Like so many other ruins in Istanbul squatters inhabit them.

The stretch of wall from *Tekfur Saray* to the Golden Horn is quite different from the Theodosian fortifications. It is a single bulwark without a moat, but to make up for this deficiency it is thicker and more massive than the main Theodosian wall, and its towers are stronger, higher and placed closer together. The Emperor Manuel Comnenus (AD 1143–80) built the first part of this section of the walls. This wall begins just beyond *Tekfur Saray*, where it starts westward almost at right angles to the last fragment of the Theodosian wall and then turns right at the third tower.

The wall of Manuel Comnenus is an admirably constructed fortification consisting of high arches closed on the outer face. It contains nine towers and one public gate, now called *Egri Kapi*. Most authorities identify *Egri Kapi* with the ancient Gate of the Kaligaria. It was here that his friend George Phrantzes,

One of the first towers in the newer wall. Emperor Manuel Comnenus (AD 1143–80) built the first part of this section of the walls. This wall begins just beyond *Tekfur Saray*, where it starts westward almost at right angles to the last fragment of the Theodosian wall and then turns right at the third tower. The wall of Manuel Comnenus is an admirably constructed fortification consisting of high arches closed on the outer face. It contains nine towers and one public gate.

the chronicler who would later write a history of the fall of Byzantium, last saw Emperor Constantine XI alive. On the night of 28 May 1453 the emperor, accompanied by Phrantzes, stopped briefly at the palace after returning from his last visit to *Haghia Sophia*. According to Phrantzes, Constantine assembled the members of his household and said goodbye to each of them in turn, asking their forgiveness for any unkindness he might ever have shown them, 'Who could describe the tears and groans in the palace?' Phrantzes wrote, 'Even a man of wood or stone could not help weeping.' The emperor then left the palace and rode with Phrantzes down to the Gate of the Kaligaria. They dismounted there and Phrantzes waited while Constantine ascended one of the towers nearby, whence he could hear the Turkish artillery preparing for the final assault. Soon after he returned and mounted his horse once again. Phrantzes then said goodbye to Constantine for the last time and watched as the emperor rode off to his command post on the *Murus Bacchatureus*, never to be seen again.

The Turkish name *Egri Kapi*, the Crooked Gate, is so called because the narrow lane that leaves the city here must detour around a tomb that stands almost directly in front of the portal. This is the supposed tomb of Hazret Hafiz, a companion of the Prophet, who, according to tradition, was killed on this spot during the first Arab siege of the city in AD 674–78. Several sainted Arab heroes of that campaign are buried in the vicinity, all having been dispatched to Paradise by the defenders on the walls of Constantinople.

From *Egri Kapi* one may continue along the path just inside the walls to see the remainder of the wall of Manuel Comnenus, which ends at the third tower past the gate. The rest of this section of wall, from the third tower to where it joins the retaining wall of the Blachernae terrace, appears to be of later construction. The workmanship here is much inferior to that in the wall of Manuel Comnenus. This can clearly be seen where the two join without bonding, just beyond the third tower from *Egri Kapi*.

Four towers, all square and also much inferior to those in the previous section, guard this section. The wall of Manuel Comnenus bears no dated

ABOVE *Egri Kapi*. Most authorities identify *Egri Kapi* with the ancient Gate of the Kaligaria. The Turkish name *Egri Kapi*, the Crooked Gate, is so called because the narrow lane that leaves the city here must detour around a tomb that stands almost directly in front of the portal.

LEFT Blachernae today, showing the ruins of the so-called Prison of Anemas in the outer circuit of the walls.

inscriptions. The later northern one has three: one dated AD 1188 by Isaac II Angelus; another AD 1311 by Andronicus II Palaeologus; and the third AD 1441 by John VIII Palaeologus. There is also in this northern section a postern, now walled up, which is thought to be the ancient Gyrolimne Gate or the 'Gate of the Silver Lake'. This was an entrance to the Palace of Blachernae, whose outer retaining wall and two towers continue the line of fortifications in this area.

The fortification from the northern corner of the Blachernae terrace to the Golden Horn consists of two parallel walls joined at their two ends to form a

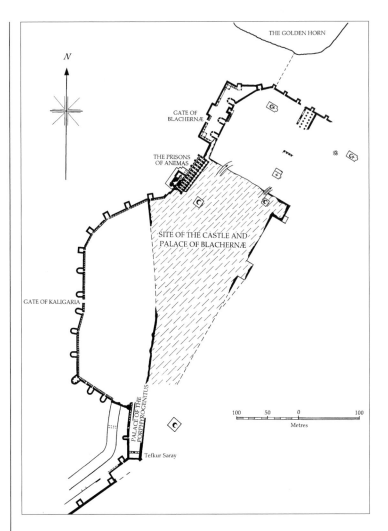

THE GOLDEN HORN

GATE OF
BLACHERNÆ

THE PRISONS
OF ANEMAS

SITE OF THE CASTLE AND
PALACE OF BLACHERNÆ

GATE OF KALIGARIA

PALACE OF THE
PORPHYROGENITUS

Tefkur Saray

100 50 0 100

Metres

N

Plan of the Blachernae Quarter, showing how the later walls spread outwards to enclose this vital strategic area. (© Copyright Osprey Publishing Limited, artwork by John Richards)

kind of citadel. The Emperor Heraclius built the inner wall in AD 627 in an attempt to strengthen the defences in this area when the city was being threatened by the Avars and the Persians. The three hexagonal defence towers in this short stretch of wall are perhaps the finest in the whole system. In AD 813, when Krum the Bulgar threatened the city, Leo V decided to strengthen the defences in this vulnerable area by building an outer wall with four small towers, a fortification thinner than the older one behind it and much inferior in construction. These walls were pierced by a single entryway, the Gate of the Blachernae. That part of the gate that passed through the wall of Leo has now collapsed, but it is still open through the Heraclian wall, passing between the first and second towers.

The Wall of Leo stands 77ft to the west of the Wall of Heraclius, running parallel to it for some 260ft, after which it turns to join the walls along the Golden Horn. Its parapet walk was supported upon arches, which served at the same time to buttress the wall itself, a comparatively slight structure about 8ft thick. In order to increase the wall's capacity for defence it was flanked by four small towers, while numerous loopholes pierced its lower portion. Two of the towers were on the side facing the Golden Horn, and the other two guarded the extremities of the side looking towards the country on the west. The latter towers projected inwards from the rear of the wall, and between them was a gateway corresponding to the Heraclian Gate of Blachernae.

In AD 1081 the friends of Alexius Comnenus sallied from the city through the Gate of Blachernae to raise the standard of revolt against Nicephorus Botoniates. It was at the imperial stables outside the gate that they obtained horses to reach as fast as possible the Monastery of SS. Cosmas and Damianus, preventing any pursuit by hamstringing the animals they did not require. In AD 1097 Godfrey de Bouillon and his crusaders encamped on the hills and plains outside this stretch of wall.

The area of the citadel between the walls of Leo and Heraclius is quite fascinating to visit and study, and has been much improved in recent years. On my visit in 1996 I noted that the ground was covered with rubble that had fallen from the walls and towers, among which there had developed a little hamlet of squatters who had built their hovels from the debris. By 2003 the area had been attractively landscaped as a public park. At the northern end of the citadel the walls of Leo and Heraclius come together and link up with the sea walls along the Golden Horn.

The living site

Strategic considerations

The maintenance and manning of the walls of Constantinople was but one small part of the overall Byzantine strategy, which had as its sole aim the defence of the empire. Byzantine military arrangements were set out in a consistent and logically well-considered manner. They recognised that the resources they had at their disposal were limited and had to work out how best to use them in the defence of the empire. This point was noted quite clearly by the mid-10th century AD by a visitor from Italy, the ambassador Liudprand of Cremona. He was also very interested in the precautions taken to secure Constantinople by night in case of a surprise enemy attack. Watch was kept from every gateway and tower, and access was at all times strictly controlled. These sorts of considerations were backed up by a vigorous diplomatic effort that was not merely aimed at avoiding the shedding of Christian blood. On the contrary, the whole future of the state, and the security of its apparently huge and mighty walls depended upon having friends to aid you and enemies whose intentions one could understand. Preparation was of the greatest importance, as the Chronicle of Theophanes reminds us for the Arab attack in AD 714:

> then the Emperor commanded each man to be able to pay his own way for three years' time, and ordered those unable to do so to abandon the city. He made sails and began to build warships, Greek-fire-carrying biremes, and huge triremes. He restored the land and sea walls, and installed arrow-shooting engines, stone-throwing engines and catapults on the gates. He stored up a great amount of produce in the imperial granaries and secured it as best he could, and strengthened the city to the best of his ability.

It is also worthy of note that there were several occasions when strategic considerations led to a siege of Constantinople's walls being abandoned as a result of a victory gained many miles away. The best example concerns the year AD 1090, when the Patzinaks, a warlike nomadic people from the plains of southern Russia, reached the walls of the capital after a series of hotly contested struggles with imperial troops. As if this was not enough, Constantinople was also assailed by sea from the fleet of Tzachas the emir of Smyrna. He had once been a prisoner of the imperial court, and that experience had shown him that any decisive blow against Constantinople had to include a movement from the sea.

In his dire need Emperor Alexius I Comnenus allied himself with another nomadic group called the Cumans, and with their help defeated the Patzinaks at the battle of Mount Levunion. The Patzinaks were completely wiped out. As Anna Comnena, Alexius' daughter and biographer, wrote, 'An entire people, numbering myriads, was exterminated on a single day.' Tzachas' seaborne blockade was neutralised and had to be abandoned. The walls of Constantinople were safe again.

The walls and the army

The walls and gates of Constantinople may have been formidable, but they always depended upon a supply of men to defend them. Although modern research has shed light on the overall organisation of the Byzantine army, much less is known about the soldiers whose job it was to guard the capital from Constantinople's walls. When danger threatened soldiers were found

This painting of the walls of Constantinople on the exterior wall of the Moldovita monastery in Romania shows the city being defended during the AD 1453 siege. Archers are operating from the top of the tower, while the emperor and empress parade on the walls with priests. (Photograph by David Nicolle)

wherever possible, and there is no evidence that divisions of garrison troops had any special names or titles, or that garrison soldiers were distinguishable from any of the mercenaries who lived in the city. The garrison would therefore appear to have consisted of any standing troops who were ready at a moment's notice to defend the walls against attack. They were distinguishable only from the palace guards.

The best example of a garrison in action in Constantinople is a group of Catalan mercenaries who were given the job of defending the Golden Gate fort on behalf of John Cantacuzenus in AD 1352. We are told that their commander Juan de Peralta had known John Cantacuzenus since their days in Serbia some years earlier, so these mercenaries can probably be identified as the group of 'Latin' or 'German' mercenaries who had deserted Stephen Dushan in Serbia.

The function of the Golden Gate garrison was twofold: to defend the city if the rival emperor John V Palaeologus attacked it and to maintain John Cantacuzenus' hold over the city. This was no idle threat. The people were warned that if they surrendered to John V Palaeologus they would face both John Cantacuzenus' Turkish allies and the garrison of the city.

There are also records of occasions when troops were sent from Constantinople to garrison other towns then under threat. For example, when Andronicus III besieged Apros in AD 1322, 220 cavalry, 200 archers and 30 crossbowmen, sent from Constantinople, reinforced the town's garrison. This was a great help to a local force that consisted of 100 cavalry, archers and slingers, and a force drawn from those living nearby who 'came together because of the war'.

The garrisoning of Constantinople, however, involved considerations that went far beyond the fighting quality of the men stationed on its walls. Defence of the capital was as much a political need as a military one, and required a delicate balancing act. Large numbers of troops in and around the capital always represented a potential threat to the emperor's safety. Hence the small numbers employed as bodyguards, and the preference for foreign troops such as the Varangian guardsmen described below. In any case, the maintenance of a large permanent garrison would have been an enormously expensive proposition. The cost of maintaining the Byzantine army was the empire's largest item of expenditure, and when there was a major threat to Constantinople regional forces could be sent to the city quite speedily.

The Varangian Guard

Of all the mercenaries employed to serve in Constantinople none are better known than the famous Varangian Guard, who were recruited from the Scandinavian north. Forging their way from their own inhospitable lands the Northmen, first of all from Sweden, reached the Volga and later by the so-called 'Varangian Way' came down from Russia by way of the Dnieper and the Black Sea to Constantinople. They came first as pirates, then as traders and finally as the most trusted guards of the Byzantine emperors. During the first half of the 11th

This interesting and evocative stretch of damaged wall lies in a section immediately to the north of the Golden Gate. Artillery was a vital factor in the fall of Constantinople in AD 1453, not merely because of the number of guns possessed by Mehmet the Conqueror, but the sensible use he made of them.

century AD Harold Hardrada served in the Varangian Guard. Later that same century in the aftermath of the Norman Conquest, many Anglo-Saxons from England joined their ranks, the earliest written record of their presence being AD 1088.

The Varangians are frequently referred to in the Byzantine chronicles as 'axe-bearing warriors'. Their axes were wielded wherever their emperor needed them, and this included service on the walls of Constantinople. The best records of the Varangians manning the walls date from the Fourth Crusade. The chronicler Nicetas Choniates tells us that when the crusaders tried to enforce a landing at the imperial pier on the Golden Horn near Blachernae they were driven back by the great bravery of the allies of the Greeks who included the Pisans and the 'axe-bearing barbarians'. Villehardouin tells us that English and Danes manned the wall, and that 'the fighting was very violent, and there was a hand to hand fight with axes and swords, the assailants mounted on the wall and prisoners were taken on both sides'. He also tells us that when the Latins sent envoys to the Emperor Isaac, Englishmen and Danes were posted at the gate of the city and all along the road to the Blachernae Palace, fully armed with their formidable axes.

The service by the Varangian Guard does not seem to have lasted much beyond the restoration of Byzantine power under Michael VIII. There is however a reference of 1329 to 'the Varangians with their axes' who were accustomed to guarding the keys of any city in which the emperor was staying. There is no mention of them in action during the sieges by the Ottomans in the 14th and 15th centuries, and the only trace of them left in Istanbul today is an interesting and unique memorial to the Varangian Guard high up in the southern gallery of the church of *Haghia Sophia*. There on a balustrade a Varangian guardsman carved his name, 'Halvdan', in Viking runes.

Water and food supply

No matter how strong a city's walls might be, its population has to be supplied with food and water, and Constantinople was no exception. The original site of Byzantium was poorly supplied with natural water sources. The stream called the Lycus that has long since disappeared once flowed into the city, and there were a few small springs. At a further distance two streams once known as the 'Sweet Waters of Europe' flowed into the Golden Horn.

The first aqueduct to bring water to Byzantium was built by the Emperor Hadrian. Records note that it soon proved inadequate, and the growing population of the new capital founded by Constantine led in AD 373 to the building of the first aqueduct to take water into the heart of the city. This was the aqueduct of Valens, named after the emperor who commissioned it. The aqueduct still stands as a striking monument in the middle of busy Istanbul, straddling a multi-lane highway. What we see today was only part of a huge network that took about 30 years to complete and was described by Gregory or Nazianzus as 'a subterranean and aerial river'.

But to bring water in is one thing. It also needed to be stored, so very large underground and surface cisterns and reservoirs were added within the city

This is the only trace of the Varangian Guard left in Istanbul today. It is a unique memorial to them and lies high up in the southern gallery of the church of *Haghia Sophia*. There on a balustrade a Varangian guardsman carved his name 'Halvdan' in Viking runes.

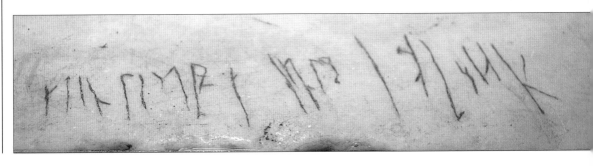

walls. In AD 626, during the siege of Constantinople by the Avars, the besiegers cut the aqueduct of Valens, but the act had no serious consequences. This was probably because the damage was slight, and also because of the storage facilities. For example, Justinian built the *Yerebatan Saray*, the huge pillared underground cistern that is one of the great sights of Istanbul, during the AD 530s. Curiously, knowledge of this colossal urban reservoir was lost in the century following the conquest by the Ottomans. It was only rediscovered in AD 1545 when Petrus Gyllius, a traveller to the city engaged upon the study of Byzantine antiquities, heard that the inhabitants of this area obtained their water supplies by lowering buckets through the floors of their houses, while some even caught fish there!

As for food supply, by AD 1200 the empire had lost its richest provinces for good, notably Egypt, once the source of grain that had fed the population up to the time of Heraclius. This could have posed serious problems, particularly when an attack loomed, but Constantinople was actually able to feed itself from its lands in Thrace and the fields round the Aegean. Ships and carts ferried the grain to Constantinople, where it was stored and distributed through a commercial network.

The aqueduct of Valens. The growing population of the new capital founded by Constantine led in AD 373 to the building of the first aqueduct to take water into the heart of the city. This was the aqueduct of Valens, named after the emperor who commissioned it. The aqueduct still stands as a striking monument in the middle of busy Istanbul, straddling a multi-lane highway.

Siege weapons and the defence of the walls

The defenders of Constantinople had several types of siege weaponry at their disposal. Various forms of catapults designed to throw stones or arrows were used both to defend Constantinople and attack it until the early 15th century, but it is not clear how much continuity there was between the Roman war machines of the 4th and 5th centuries AD and the later Byzantine weapons. The classic Roman model was the two-armed horizontally mounted torsion-powered catapult. This was a device that required considerable technical knowledge and expertise both to produce and maintain. The crucial factor of having equivalent torsion levels in both springs required great mathematical and engineering knowledge, and this does not appear to have been available in abundance from the 5th and 6th centuries AD onwards. Instead the Byzantine historian Procopius described the use of the *onager*, the familiar Roman torsion catapult that used one vertical arm threaded through some form of torsion spring in a horizontal plane. Such machines could throw stones and incendiary missiles. They had the disadvantage of having to be constructed very solidly to give the stability they needed to operate, but these skills were generally available. The *Tactica* of Leo tells of field artillery units that accompanied the infantry. They were wagon-mounted and with a single pole, which rules out the two-armed torsion catapults. At the siege of Adrianople by the Goths in AD 378 the defenders hurled a huge stone ball from

The sea walls of Constantinople and a Byzantine ship armed with a Greek fire projector c. AD 1000

The sea walls were never as strong as the land walls, but served their purpose when well defended. Here we see two elements in that defence. The first is Greek fire, the secret weapon of Byzantium, seen being tested here from the deck of a *dromon* just outside the Harbour of Bucoleon on the Sea of Marmara. The performance is being watched from the battlements by the Varangian Guards. Their famous axes were wielded wherever their emperor needed them, and this included service on the walls of Constantinople.

Haghia Eirene

Haghia Sofia

Church of SS Sergius and Bacchus

38

an *onager* against a densely packed group of Goths. No damage was done, but the incident caused considerable alarm and impressed the besiegers.

The Byzantines also used machines that projected bolts or arrows. Procopius again describes these, and the language he uses to illustrate their operation implies that they were not torsion devices but received their stored energy from tension. As words for bow appear in the long names he uses for the weapons some form of siege crossbow is more than likely. Procopius also gives a good indication of the force that could be mounted behind the flight of one of these bolts. During Vitiges' siege of Rome in AD 536 a bolt hit a Goth as he sat halfway up a tree, shooting arrows from a hand bow. The bolt nailed him to the tree and he hung there, pinned to the trunk!

While the one-armed *onager* seems to have survived under the Byzantine Empire, the Avars introduced other stone-throwing weapons in the late 6th century AD. These were based neither on torsion nor tension, but made use of the energy given to a lever by a team of men pulling ropes in unison. These were the traction trebuchets, the forerunners of the later and larger counterweight trebuchets that did not make their appearance in Western Europe until the late 13th century. The traction trebuchet originated in China and had travelled west. Counterweight trebuchets would certainly have played a part in the defences of Constantinople once their use had been established after the Crusades.

Gunpowder weapons at Constantinople

By the last two decades of the 14th century the Byzantines had begun to accumulate gunpowder weapons, spurred on by the growing threat on their doorstep posed by the Ottomans. The earliest were medium-sized cannon about 3ft in length and with a calibre up to 10in. Only a few large bombards were to be found in Byzantine arsenals. By the middle of the 15th century handguns also began to appear.

This staircase in the inner wall is being rebuilt and shows very clearly the use of brick and stone. It is also a welcome indication that the most recent rebuilding work is being done sensitively and well.

In 1390 there took place a *coup d'etat* that resulted in the emperor John V Palaeologus being besieged in the Golden Gate fortress by his grandson John VII Cantacuzenus. This incident is interesting because it may have involved the earliest use of gunpowder weapons at Constantinople, but the actual passage in the chronicles is ambiguous, as it refers to the attackers 'beating' against the walls. Guns are first definitely mentioned when Bayezid the Thunderbolt's Turks came along to besiege the city in 1396. The Ottomans had no firearms of their own but made use of conventional siege machinery such as trebuchets. The defenders, however, did possess cannon, although the source tells of them being used by the 'Franks' (probably the Genoese) of Galata, and that the noise and smoke they produced, together with crossbow bolts and stones from slings, caused the Turks to withdraw. These cannon may therefore have been Genoese weapons that were not under the control of the Byzantine forces.

By the time of the siege of 1422, a fight that was to be the dress rehearsal for 1453, the Turks had their own artillery, and in a major eyewitness source about this siege John Kananos describes how the Turks used 'falcons' (short fat cannons) along with other siege weapons such as 'tortoises', the covered wagons used to protect miners. The defenders had cannon too, so the Turks built barricades 'in order to receive the arrows of the bows and of the crossbows of the Romans, and the stones of the bombards'. The Byzantines had roughly the same level of technology as the Ottomans, although the eventual lifting of the 1422 siege was credited not to the success of the Byzantine artillery, but to the miraculous intervention of the Virgin herself, who appeared on the walls and inspired the defenders.

Such apparitions had saved Constantinople in the past, but it would be an exaggeration to blame such touching faith for the extraordinary fact that during the next 30 years the Byzantines do not seem to have made any progress in developing their artillery. Nor did they attempt to remodel any part of their huge medieval walls to withstand a possible bombardment on a contemporary scale. The reasons for such failures are probably very mundane ones of Constantinople's severe economic problems, which led to a simple shortage of cash to buy the guns or to hire the experts who could both cast and use them. Indeed, many of the cannon that were eventually used to defend Constantinople during the siege of AD 1453 appear to have been made available to them as gifts, a practice promoted later by Pope Pius II as a way of helping the Byzantines. It was a gesture that most crowned heads of Europe could easily afford, and it was also a safer alternative to going on crusade to provide military help to Constantinople.

Economic problems just before the fateful siege of AD 1453 were partly to blame for the well-known story (recounted originally by the chronicler Dukas) that tells how a Hungarian artillery expert named Urban approached the Byzantine emperor with an offer to cast guns for the defence of the city. This was the opportunity for which the defenders of Constantinople had been waiting, but because the price he demanded was too high he was sent away. Urban immediately turned to Sultan Mehmet II, who hired him for four times the fee he had asked. Urban's creations were the two giant bombards. He had boasted that these cannon could reduce 'even the walls of Babylon'. They took three months to make and were test fired at Adrianople (Edirne), where:

> public announcements were made ... to advise everyone of the loud and thunderous noise which it would make so that no one would be struck dumb by hearing the noise unexpectedly or any pregnant women miscarry.

The enormous cannon were each transported to Constantinople by 70 oxen and 10,000 men. Following the advice of his artillerymen, Mehmet II positioned his siege guns against the weakest and most vulnerable parts of the wall. The

targets included the imperial palace of Blachernae at the north-western corner of the city and the Gate of St Romanus in the middle wall. The bombardment, which was to last 55 days, soon began to cause massive destruction, and the chronicler Kritovoulos has left a fascinating description of what happened when one of the enormous stone balls hit its target:

> And the stone, borne with enormous force and velocity, hit the wall, which it immediately shook and knocked down, and was itself broken into many fragments and scattered, hurling the pieces everywhere and killing those who happened to be nearby.

From the Byzantine side the defenders hit back with their own artillery weapons. The available guns were distributed along the walls and used as required, either against Turkish siege machinery or as anti-personnel weapons together with crossbows. As Dukas recounts:

> [These guns] fired, with the help of powder, five or ten bullets at a time, each about the size of a Pontic walnut, and having a great power of penetration. If one of these hit an armed man, it would go right through his shield and his body, and go on to hit anyone else who happened to be in his way, and even a third until the force of the powder diminished. So one shot might kill two or three men.

There was some initial success as the Byzantines settled down to the effects of the Turkish bombardment. Soon they could repel whatever siege engine they could see, reports Leonard of Chios, but the Turks responded by hiding their war machines from view. The Byzantine artillery faced several other problems, one of the most serious being that the flat roofs of the towers in the medieval walls were not sufficiently strong to act as gun emplacements. As Leonard of Chios put it, 'the largest cannon had to remain silent for fear of damage to our own walls by vibration'. Chalkondylas even wrote that the act of firing cannon did more harm to the towers than the Turkish bombardment. Even the largest of the Byzantine cannon was smaller than the Turkish equivalents, and when it burst a great fury rose against the artilleryman. He was suspected of having been bribed by the Sultan and would have been executed, but was finally released for lack of evidence.

Greek fire

Greek fire was the secret weapon of the Byzantine Empire. Its introduction can be dated quite exactly, because Theophanes, who finished his *Chronographia* in AD 815, described how the Arabs continually attacked Constantinople from AD 674 to 678, but finally gave up. One factor in this was the chemical process introduced a few years earlier by an architect-cum-engineer called Callinicus that produced Greek fire. Incendiaries using naturally occurring mineral oils

The sea wall on the Sea of Marmara just below the Topkapi Palace. The entrance to the Golden Horn lies round the corner. The simpler construction of the sea walls compared to the Theodosian walls can be seen.

had been known about for some time. Naphtha, for example, was obtained by the filtration of crude oil. The particular feature of Greek fire that made it so revolutionary and so much a state secret, was that it used petroleum that had been distilled, although many of the accounts of so-called naphtha-throwing may also involve what was actually distilled petrol.

Most accounts of Greek fire in the defence of Constantinople are to do with naval warfare. The burning petrol would float on the surface of the sea and destroy the hulls of enemy ships. It would, however, dissipate rather quickly and carry only a short distance. For this reason it was thickened with resinous substances. The means of delivery in Constantinople was by siphons, which were effectively ancient flamethrowers. These siphons were mounted on Byzantine ships, and were often given the shapes of animal heads at the ends of the tubes. Emperor Leo's *Tactica*, written in the 8th or 9th century AD, tells us how the men who worked the bronze flame-throwing pumps were protected by iron shields, and that the blazing jets, which may have been of a considerable size, made the noise of rumbling thunder. Smaller handheld versions also apparently existed. One account says that the pumps were worked by compressed air, which could mean that the petrol was forced out using some sort of piston-bellows. Another implies that flexible pipes formed part of the overall apparatus, because the siphon could be directed to left or right at the will of the operator, or even at a high elevation to fall on to the enemy ships from above.

The repulse of the Arab sieges of Constantinople involved Byzantine ships sailing out of Constantinople and attacking them with Greek fire. A later large-scale use took place during the Russian attack on Constantinople in AD 941:

> The Greeks began to fling their fire all around; and the Rus, seeing the flames, threw themselves in haste from their ships, preferring to be drowned in the water rather than burned alive in the fire.

The Greek fire projectors were mounted on a swivel so that they could be aimed in any direction. A good example of seaborne use is AD 1103 when Emperor Alexius Comnenus used Greek fire against the Pisans near Rhodes.

Greek fire could also be used against troops on land or to set fire to siege weapons. There are not many references to this, but it is interesting to note the employment of Greek fire during the final siege of Constantinople in AD 1453.

It was used on one occasion then as a defensive weapon for a ship arriving with grain. Turkish attempts to intercept it were beaten off using Greek fire. It was also very useful against siege towers. We are told that a German, reportedly named Johann Grant, directed the fire. He sprayed Greek fire on to an enormous siege machine, presumably a belfry lined inside and outside with three layers of ox hide. The machine had already helped bring down the tower of St Romanus during the night, but the defenders repaired it very quickly, astounding the Sultan by their endeavours.

Greek fire was also used when the Ottoman soldiers stormed the walls. Fire was poured down on to the unfortunate souls climbing up, and we are given a nightmare picture of the soldiers falling into the moat screaming with pain. The maces and whips of guards beat more of these forlorn hope troops forward, while the Janissaries in the background cut down any who fled. But by AD 1453 gunpowder was the decisive weapon, and attempts to use Greek fire from ships against the Turkish troops were cut short by cannon fire. It was the end of an era in more ways than one.

Further detail concerning Greek fire has come from the fact that its use eventually spread as far as China and entered the repertoire of Chinese siegecraft around AD 900. A detailed description of the Chinese version is given in the *Wu Jing Zong Yao* of AD 1044. Chinese illustrations are also more detailed and realistic than Byzantine ones, and show that the Chinese Greek fire container was made of brass and fitted with a horizontal pump, which terminated in the gunpowder ignition chamber, and a small-diameter nozzle. When the handle was pushed in and out vigorously petrol was squirted out. It is unlikely that Byzantine ones were much different, and the Chinese author recommends placing these machines on the ramparts or the outworks of cities. An excellent account of the Chinese use of Greek fire concerns a battle on the Yangtze near Nanjing in AD 975 between the Song and the Tang, where things did not quite go according to plan because 'he quickly projected petrol from flame throwers to destroy the enemy. The Song forces could not have withstood this, but all of a sudden a north wind sprang up and swept the smoke and flames over the sky towards his own ships and men'. It was a scenario that may well have happened in the Byzantine Empire.

The supernatural defenders of Constantinople

A western traveller to Constantinople early in the 15th century AD surmised that God had spared the city more for the holy relics it contained than for anything else. It was a perceptive observation, because the city's inhabitants

The Virgin Mary was honoured as Constantinople's greatest protector, stronger than any wall or weapon. Here she is depicted in a mosaic in the gallery of *Haghia Sophia*. Dressed in purple, the colour of the robe in which she was seen in visions on the walls, she is holding the Christ Child. She is flanked by portraits of Emperor John II Comnenus, who reigned from AD 1118 to 1143 and his wife the Empress Eirene.

This is the largest surviving section of sea wall on the Golden Horn. Most of the other sea walls in this area have been destroyed by modern development.

believed that they enjoyed the protection of a secret weapon even more potent than Greek fire. This was the firm belief that God and his saints provided supernatural help, and one particular way in which their spiritual help was guaranteed lay in the possession of relics. The body of St Stephen the first martyr, the head of John the Baptist and the leather tunic of the pillar-dwelling St Symeon Stylites all had their sanctuaries within Constantinople along with numerous other relics of saints. In AD 944 as a result of his victories John Curcuas carried to Constantinople the famous portrait of Christ believed to have been painted by St Luke, which had been granted to Abgar, King of Edessa. It was recorded that by this act 'Constantinople would thereby acquire greater strength and would be kept for all time unharmed and unravaged'.

But of all the supernatural defenders of Constantinople none were held in more esteem or relied on more fully than the Blessed Virgin Mary, the *Theotokos* (Mother of God). Constantinople was her city and the churches dedicated to her outnumbered all others. The most important of all these churches was the one at Blachernae that originally lay outside the Theodosian walls but was later enclosed for safety. During the 5th century AD Constantinople acquired its most precious relic in the form of the robe of the Virgin. The city also possessed her shroud, her girdle and the swaddling clothes in which Jesus had been wrapped. In the succession of perils to which the walls of Constantinople were subjected their ultimate salvation was invariably ascribed to the protection of the Mother of God. Any reverses such as burning of outer suburbs by attackers were explained a God's punishment for sins. Prayers were then offered to the Virgin, and these appeared to save the city time and time again.

The most touching images of the Virgin as the protectress of Constantinople concern her miraculous appearance on the city's mighty walls. Icons bearing her image were paraded round the walls in time of siege, and in times of direst need she was seen standing on the walls and inspiring the defenders. Such an incident allowed the chronicler to place an excuse for failure into the mouth of the besieging Avars in the *Chronicon Pascale* account of the siege of AD 626: 'And this is what the godless Chagan said at the moment of the battle: "I see a woman in a stately dress rushing about on the wall all alone."' In accounts of other sieges there was usually a focal point of one of the relics of the Virgin, such as in AD 860 when the Virgin's robe was dipped into the sea.

Gratitude to the Virgin Mary is described by John Kananos in his account of the 1422 siege. On that occasion she had appeared on the walls during an attack, and greatly inspired the defenders:

> The Romans, though exhausted from fatigue, leapt and were glad. They clapped their hands and rendered special thanks to God. They shouted hymns to the Most Holy Virgin, glorifying her from the depths of their hearts, saying, 'This is in truth a rich, celebrated, memorable, extraordinary and remarkable miracle worthy of admiration.'

The miracle was even confirmed by the enemy:

> The army of the Turks confirmed by an oath sworn to Mersaites, spoken of by all at the hour of battle, that on arriving at the walls of the city with an

irresistible force to scale them and pursue the Romans and conquer the city, they saw a woman dressed in purple robes walking on the ramparts of the outer fortifications, and having seen her shudders and fright immediately entered everybody's soul. So because of the woman fear overtook them and the city was liberated.

As will be recounted below, Kananos noted that that the women of Constantinople were very active in the defence, approaching near enough to the 'front line' to get hit by arrows, so the apparition may just have been an interpretation put upon an action of some brave wife or sister. However, it is by no means improbable that the Turks should seize upon an apparition of the Virgin as an honourable excuse for their failure to take the city.

The role of the citizens

When danger threatened it was not only the mercenaries in the city or the palace guard that rushed to its defence. All accounts indicate that the ordinary inhabitants rallied round, and there is no better illustration than the story of how the walls of Constantinople were defended during the siege of AD 1422 by citizens as well as soldiers, as related by John Kananos:

The volley of arrows fired at the ramparts darkened the sky and forced all the defenders to duck for cover, thus giving the Turks the impression that their ploy had actually succeeded in clearing the walls at one go. Siege towers were wheeled forwards, and scaling ladders flung against the towers. Who in fact did not tremble at that hour? Who did not shiver at the sight? Which ear could stand the sound, which eye the spectacle?

writes John Kananos, but then a miracle happened, and a change of heart came over the defenders.

They led each other out from their hiding places, for, those who formerly were fainthearted or fleeing, were unexpectedly transformed into brave and noble warriors who despised both blows and ugly wounds, and by the hope of the Most Holy Virgin they armed themselves with swords and stones and fell upon the godless plunderers. Even as smoke disperses a swarm of bees, one encouraged another, every person and age group with the weapons they had, some even with just their hands, others with swords and staves. They fastened ropes to the platters off which they had been eating their food, or the ends of barrels, and used them as shields. Some even went to fight without these but fought bravely and with valour armed only with stones as if they were wearing a complete suit of armour.

Here, for John Kananos, the religious motivation takes over completely. They encourage each other to fight 'especially for the true faith of the Christian'. They talk of throwing themselves into battle 'as the martyrs ran into the stadia of the tyrants'. They fought furiously 'as if drunk', and after a tremendous struggle drove the Turkish army back off the walls, decapitating a few unfortunates whom they caught on ladders and presenting the heads to the emperor. All the townspeople joined in, including priests and monks, and many women:

They came as far as the outer fortifications, and some carried stones up to the walls for the fighting Romans and encouraged them ... Others took eggs and cloth to treat the injuries, while others would give a drink of water and wine to those who were burning with thirst from the fatigue of combat ... some were struck by missiles and suffered wounds.

The peribolos between the outer and inner walls, AD 1422

The inner terrace between the inner and outer walls was called the *peribolos*, and accommodated the soldiers who defended the outer wall. It was between 50 and 64ft wide. Beyond lay the outer wall, which was a modest structure compared with the inner wall. This plate shows a memorable moment during the Ottoman siege of AD 1422. An apparition of the Virgin Mary on the wall has heartened the citizens.

The walls of Constantinople under siege

All the designs, all the precautions and prayers, all the strategies of defence of the great walls of Constantinople were put to the test on several memorable occasions during the city's long history when enemies placed the city under siege. In this section we will examine each of the major sieges of Constantinople using primary source materials to see how the walls played their part in the defence of the city. Usually attacks were directed against the land walls, but the sea walls also came under threat. In addition to the incidents listed below there are also other examples of Constantinople changing hands during wars between rival emperors, but none of these actions involved prolonged sieges. The pattern then tended to be that of opportunism or treachery, as for example when Alexius Comnenus entered the city with the connivance of German mercenaries stationed in the capital. Three days of plunder and riot followed.

The siege by the Avars and Persians – AD 626

The mighty appearance of the walls alone acted as a sufficient deterrent to drive back Attila the Hun in the 4th century AD. The siege of the city by the Avars and Persians in AD 626 therefore became the first test ever placed upon the walls of Constantinople. It was also one of the most severe encounters. The Persians had overrun all the Roman provinces in the Near East and were now allied with the Avars, who were steadily dominating the Balkans. Constantinople was well prepared to withstand the siege for which the Avars were preparing a huge operation. The Avars also possessed the most up-to-date siege engines in the form of traction trebuchets. These originated from China, and their first use in the European theatre is recorded in Thessalonica in AD 586. They also had mobile armoured shelters (the medieval 'sows') and siege towers, the latter covered in hides for fire protection. The shelters were deployed around the walls when the Avars arrived on 29 July. On 31 July an attack was launched along the entire length of the Theodosian walls, but the main effort was concentrated against the central section, particularly the low-lying *mesoteichion*. More siege engines were brought up. Some had been constructed from prefabricated parts brought by the invaders, augmented by timber stripped from buildings near the ramparts. The *Chronicon Paschale* gives us a vivid account of the operation:

And again on the following day he stationed a multitude of siege engines close to each other against that part which had been attacked by him, so that those in the city were compelled to station very many siege engines inside the wall. When the infantry battle was joined each day, through the efficacy of God, as a result of their superiority our men kept off the enemy at a distance. But he bound together his stone-throwers and covered them outside with hides; and in the section from the Polyandrion gate as far as the gate of St Romanus he prepared to station 12 lofty siege towers, which were advanced almost as far as the outworks, and he covered them with hides.

The Avars were soon joined by the Persians, but instead of providing the knock-out blow a blockade of the Bosphorus by the Byzantine fleet rendered them helpless spectators until the siege finished. The decisive moment occurred not on the walls but in the waters of the Golden Horn when a planned landing was intercepted. The victory was nonetheless ascribed to the protection of the Virgin Mary, one of whose principal churches lay at Blachernae, where the main fighting took place. On the night of 7–8 August the Avars burned their siege engines and the fires lit up the night sky. The walls of Constantinople had survived their first test.

The siege by the Arabs – AD 674–678

In the year AD 674 Constantinople faced a new threat from armies marching for the first time in the name of Islam. Reference has already been made to the crucial role played during this epic siege by Greek fire, but there were also assaults on the Theodosian walls. Unable to breach them, the Arabs pillaged up and down both sides of the Bosphorus and blockaded the city. But as winter approached they withdrew to an island 80 miles away. From this base they raided Constantinople for the next six years, but the city remained uncaptured. Among those killed in the attacks was Eyup, the standard bearer to the Prophet and the last surviving of his companions. His tomb is one of the holiest Muslim sites in Istanbul.

The siege by the Arabs – AD 714

More Muslim armies returned in AD 714, and the account of it mentions attacks on the walls:

> Maslama had drawn up the Muslims in a line (I had never seen a longer) with the many squadrons. Leo, the autocrat of Rum, [i.e the Emperor] sat on the tower of the gate of Constantinople with its towers. He drew up the foot soldiers in a long line between the wall and the sea opposite the Muslim line. We showed arms in a thousand ships, light ships, big ships in which were stores of Egyptian clothing, etc., and galleys with the fighting men. Laith said 'I never saw a day more amazing for our advance by land and sea, the display of our arms, the display by the autocrat of Rum on the wall of Constantinople and their array of this armament. They set up mangonels and onagers. The Muslims advanced by land and sea, the Rum showed the same [tactics] and fled disgracefully.' Urnar and some of those from the ships were afraid to advance against the harbour mouth, fearing for their lives. When the Rum saw this, galleys and light ships came out from the harbour mouth against us and one of them went to the nearest Muslim ship, threw on it grapnels with chains and towed it with its crew into Constantinople. We lost heart.

The siege by Krum the Bulgar – AD 813

In the year AD 811 Emperor Nicephorus I was killed in battle against the Bulgars under their ruthless leader Krum. Krum added insult to injury by making a drinking cup out of the emperor's skull. Two years later Krum appeared outside the Golden Gate, where he intimidated the garrison by performing human sacrifices in their sight. There was no serious attack on the walls at this time, because Emperor Leo V suggested negotiation. The two leaders were to meet beyond the walls at the northern end in front of the walls of Heraclius. Both parties were to come unarmed, but Leo had placed three bowmen in ambush. Something warned Krum the all was not well and he escaped. His wounds were superficial, but he returned to Bulgaria swearing vengeance. He was unable to carry out his threats as he died soon afterwards.

The siege by the Russians – AD 860

According to the Patriarch Photius, an eyewitness to the events, the Russian attack of AD 860 was swift and absolutely unexpected 'as a swarm of wasps'. The Russians had picked their moment well, because the emperor and his army were fighting the Arabs in Asia Minor, and the fleet was absent fighting the Arabs and Normans in the Aegean and Mediterranean. This exceptional double advantage by both land and sea suggests that the Russians may have been informed of the situation, especially the absence of the fleet. The land defence of the capital was also weakened, because the imperial army that was fighting against the Arabs consisted not only of the troops stationed in Asia Minor but also of those regiments that were usually stationed in the neighbourhood of the capital and could therefore most easily rally to its defence. The coasts of the Black Sea, the Bosphorus, and the Sea of Marmara, including its islands, were almost defenceless and helplessly exposed to Russian attacks. In the event deliverance from the Russian threat was once more attributed to the intercession of the Virgin Mary. Having hurried back to the capital, the emperor took the relic of the robe of the Virgin Mary from the church at Blachernae. It was paraded round the walls and then symbolically dipped into the sea. Immediately after this was done a strong wind arose and the ships of the 'godless Russians' were wrecked.

Attacks and sieges during the First Crusade – AD 1097

The frustrated soldiers of the First Crusade who had to pass by the great, and to them mysterious, city on their way to the Holy Land made an assault on the walls of Constantinople. While negotiations with the crafty Alexius Comnenus were proceeding, the envoys of the crusaders were on one occasion detained so long by the emperor as to arouse suspicions of treachery on his part. A band of crusaders rushed from the camp, and in their attempt to enter the city and rescue their comrades set fire to the Gate of Blachernae. The incident is recounted in the *Alexiad* of Anna Comnenus:

> A false rumour reached the others that the Counts had been thrown into prison by the Emperor. Immediately numerous regiments moved on Byzantium, and to begin with they demolished the palace near the so-called Silver Lake. They also made an attack on the walls of Byzantium, not with siege-engines indeed, as they had none, but trusting to their numbers they actually had the impudence to try to set fire to the gate below the palace which is close to the chapel built long ago by one of the Emperors to the memory of Nicolas, the greatest saint in the hierarchy.

Attacks and sieges during the Fourth Crusade – AD 1204

Tragedy struck the walls of Constantinople when more crusaders returned a century later. The notorious Fourth Crusade of AD 1204 was the only occasion prior to the fall of the city to the Ottomans in AD 1453 that the walls were breached. The Fourth Crusade had originally been designed to conquer Egypt, but after the failure of the Third Crusade there was little interest in Europe for another crusade against Islam. The Fourth Crusade, summoned by Pope Innocent III in AD 1198, was the last of the major crusades to be directed by the papacy. The later crusades were directed by individual monarchs, and even the Fourth quickly fell out of papal control.

By AD 1201 the crusader army had gathered at Venice. The Venetians had agreed a fixed fee for transporting the army by sea, but far fewer crusaders had turned up than was expected. Venice would not let the crusaders leave without being paid the full amount agreed to originally. So the Doge Dandolo made a deal and had the crusaders attack Zara, a former Venetian possession in Dalmatia. By chance, a request then came for the crusaders to aid Alexius Angelus, the son of the recently deposed Byzantine emperor Isaac II, to claim his throne. So the army turned towards Constantinople.

Golden Horn

Wall of Leo

The Gate of Blachernae

The walls in the Blachernae quarter, AD 1204

Here we have the later walls around the Blachernae quarter as the besieging crusaders would have seen them in AD 1204. The fortification from the northern corner of the Blachernae terrace to the Golden Horn consists of two parallel walls joined at their two ends to form a kind of citadel. The Emperor Heraclius built the inner wall in AD 627. In AD 813, when Krum the Bulgar threatened the city, Leo V decided to strengthen the defences in this vulnerable area by building an outer wall with four small towers. These walls were pierced by a single entryway, the Gate of the Blachernae. To the right we see the so-called Prison of Anemas.

Palace of Blachernae

Tower of Isaac Angelus

...mas

Possibly the finest restored section of the Theodosian walls lies here to the north of the Belgrade Gate. The complete system of inner wall, towers, *peribolos*, outer wall, outer walkway, small parapet and moat are shown here.

The Crusaders were still reluctant to attack fellow Christians, but the clergy convinced them that the Orthodox Byzantines were the next best thing to the Muslims. Unfortunately for them, Alexius Angelus had overstated his importance and it was quickly discovered when the crusaders arrived at the walls of Constantinople that the citizens preferred a usurper to an emperor supported by the hated 'Latins'. The crusaders and Venetians decided to place Alexius on the throne by force, and an unsuccessful amphibious assault was launched on the city in AD 1203. Twenty warships, the pathetic remains of the Byzantine navy, were sunk and the weight of the crusaders' navy broke the massive chain across the Golden Horn. Siege positions were taken up on the hill overlooking the Blachernae quarter. Assault was made with catapults and scaling ladders from ships in the Golden Horn:

> the Doge of Venice had not omitted to do his part, but had drawn up all his ships in battle formation in a line extending some three crossbow shots in length. Next the Venetians began to draw near to that part of the shore lying under the walls and towers. Then you could see their mangonels hurling stones from the decks of warships and transports, bolts from their crossbows flying across the water, archers loosing shower after shower of arrows, and the Greeks on their side fiercely defending the city from the top of its battlements, as the scaling ladders on the ships came so near that in many places swords and lances clashed one against the other. The din was so tremendous that it seemed as if both land and sea were crumbling in pieces. The galleys, however, did not dare come to shore.

The Crusaders attacked the city the following year, again initially by sea:

> Thereupon [8 April 1204], the enemy's largest ships, carrying the scaling ladders that had been readied and as many of the siege engines as had been

A view of the Golden Horn, Constantinople's fine natural harbour that was of vital strategic importance. We are looking up towards ancient Constantinople (the 'old city') from a ship docked in the Golden Horn on the Galata side. (Photograph by Eileen Brayshaw)

prepared, moved out from the shore, and, like the tilting beam of a scale's balance, they sailed over to the walls to take up positions at sufficient intervals from one another. They occupied the region extending in a line from the Monastery of Evergetes to the palace in Blachernae,which had been set on fire, the buildings within razed to the ground, thus stripping it of every pleasant spectacle.

The crusaders were eventually able to knock holes in the walls small enough for a few knights at a time to crawl through; the Venetians were also successful at scaling the walls from the sea, though there was extremely bloody fighting with the Varangians.

Two men on one of the scaling ladders nearest the Petria Gate, which was raised with great difficulty opposite the emperor, trusting themselves to fortune, were the first from among their comrades to leap down onto the tower facing them. When they drove off in alarm the Roman auxiliaries on watch, they waved their hands from above as a sign of joy and courage to embolden their countrymen. While they were jumping onto the tower, a knight by the name of Peter entered through the gate situated there. He was deemed most capable of driving in rout all the battalions, for he was nearly nine fathoms tall [54ft] and wore on his head a helmet fashioned in the shape of a towered city.

The crusaders captured the Blachernae area and used it as a base to attack the rest of the city, but while attempting to defend themselves with a wall of fire, they ended up burning down even more of the city than they had the first time. Eventually, the crusaders were victorious, and inflicted a horrible and savage sacking on Constantinople for three days, during which many ancient works of art were stolen or destroyed.

When they reached the Golden Gate of the Land walls, they pulled down the new built wall there, ran forth, and dispersed, deservedly taking the road to perdition and utter destruction. The enemy, now that there was no

This is another restored section near the Silivri Gate, known in Byzantium as the Pege Gate, or the Gate of the Spring. The contrast between the modern additions and the ancient masonry are of course very marked.

one to raise a hand against them, ran everywhere and drew the sword against every age and sex. Each did not join with the next man to form a coherent battle array, but all poured out and scattered, since everyone was terrified of them.

The sieges by the Ottomans – AD 1396, 1422 and 1453

Reference was made earlier to the AD 1396 siege by Bayezid the Thunderbolt. The role of the walls during the AD 1422 siege, so eloquently described by John Kananos, has been adequately covered above. When the Ottomans returned in AD 1453 they were much better armed and prepared because Mehmet II had made careful and well-considered plans to lay siege to Constantinople. His previous strategy of isolating the city from all sides was intensified, and he captured all the remaining Byzantine possessions on the Black Sea coast, as well as ensuring he had full command of the sea. During previous sieges Constantinople had been able to receive supplies by ship, and as recently as the Varna campaign of 1444 the Turkish army had depended upon Genoese help to cross the Bosphorus. Steps were now taken to make both these factors irrelevant in the campaign that lay ahead.

On the Asiatic shore of the Bosphorus lay a Turkish fortress called *Anadolu Hisar*. Mehmet now built another castle opposite it on the European side of the straits. Named first 'the cutter of the straits' or 'the cutter of the throat', and later simply as *Rumeli Hisar* (the European castle), the new fortress was completed in August 1452. It allowed the Ottoman artillery to control all shipping in and out of the Black Sea in a way never before possible. The

The Theodosian walls are bombarded by Mehmet the Conqueror, AD 1453
Here we view the walls of Constantinople from the outside showing the bombardment by Mehmet the Conqueror in AD 1453. The Byzantine emperor had concentrated his troops between the inner and outer walls. It was the low-lying *mesoteichion* section of the walls across the Lycus Valley that was finally breached by the Turks.

The Blachernae section of walls, showing the wall of Leo and the Gate of Blachernae. This was the main view of Constantinople that was seen by the crusaders in AD 1204, who encamped on a hill opposite.

building of the castle amounted to a declaration of war, and neither military nor diplomatic threats dissuaded Mehmet from exploiting its position. In November 1452 a Venetian galley was sunk by a cannon ball fired from *Rumeli Hisar*. The days of relief armies arriving by sea were over.

In March 1453 an Ottoman fleet assembled off Gallipoli and sailed proudly into the Sea of Marmara while the Turkish army assembled in Thrace. The sight of the Ottoman navy passing the sea walls of Constantinople towards *Rumeli Hisar* while the army approached its land walls was one that struck terror into the inhabitants. To add to the lesson already delivered from *Rumeli Hisar* concerning the potential of the Turkish artillery, Urban's cannon soon came lumbering into view. On 20 April there occurred one of the few pieces of good fortune that the defenders experienced during the entire siege when three supply ships braved the Turkish blockade and entered the Golden Horn. This natural harbour, across which the chain had been slung, was the only sea area that the Byzantines still controlled. But two days later the defenders' elation turned to despair when Mehmet II put into motion an extraordinary feat of military engineering. A wooden roadway was constructed from the Bosphorus to a stream called the Springs that entered the Golden Horn, and with much muscular effort some 80 Turkish ships were dragged overland and relaunched far beyond the boom. Seaborne attacks could now be launched from much closer quarters.

Dukas describes the final dispositions of the defenders on the walls in these words:

[The Byzantines] inside the walls were also drawn up in battle array. The emperor, with John Giustiniani, defended the walls already breached outside the fortress in the surrounding area, having with him Latins and Romans [Byzantines] in the number of about 3,000, while the grand duke

had with him about 500 men at the Imperial Gate. The walls ... were defended by more than 500 siege engines and archers. In the area from the Beautiful Gate, forming an entire circle up to the Golden Gate, in each tower there was an armed man who was either an archer, a siege engine operator, or a stone-thrower.

Rumours concerning the approach of a relieving army from Hungary prompted Mehmet II to launch a simultaneous assault against the land and sea walls on Tuesday 29 May, and the attack began in the early hours of the morning. The Byzantine emperor had concentrated his troops between the inner and outer walls, and when they were in position the gates of the inner wall were closed because there was to be no retreat. The Turkish irregulars went in first but were driven back, as were the Anatolian infantry who followed them. It was the low-lying *mesoteichion* section of the walls across the Lycus Valley that was finally breached by the Turks on the morning of 29 May 1453. A giant Janissary named Hasan, who fought his way up onto one of the towers of the outer wall, led the final charge. Hasan himself was slain, but his companions then forced their way across the *peribolos* and over the inner wall into the city, and within hours Constantinople was to fall to the Turks. A final attack by the Janissaries took the middle wall, and when a wounded senior commander of Constantinople was seen being evacuated through the inner wall into the city the impression was given that he was retreating. Resistance began to fade, and when the emperor was killed in a brave counterattack Constantinople fell. The great walls that had held out for so long were finally and irrevocably overcome.

One of the most extraordinary features of the AD 1453 siege concerned Mehmet the Conqueror's successful effort to overcome the chain across the Golden Horn. He dragged his ships overland and launched them into the waters of the Golden Horn beyond the chain.

Aftermath

The walls beyond AD 1453

Many ruined sections of the walls today are as they were left after the Ottoman guns had done their damage. The major addition made to the walls of Constantinople by the Ottomans was the creation of the Yedikule fortress at its southern end. Yedikule fortress is a curious structure, part Byzantine and part Ottoman. The seven towers that give it its name consist of four in the Theodosian walls itself, plus three additional towers built inside the walls by Mehmet the Conqueror in AD 1457. Yedikule in fact represents the only attempt by the Ottoman conquerors of Constantinople to enhance the fortifications of the city. The three inner towers are connected and joined to the Theodosian walls by four heavy curtain walls to form a five-sided enclosure.

Many buildings suffered during the final siege. The close proximity to the walls caused the Palace of the Porphyrogenitus to be badly damaged in the last siege, but after the conquest it was repaired and used for a variety of purposes. During the 16th and 17th centuries it served as an imperial menagerie particularly for larger and tamer animals such as elephants and giraffes. The latter particularly amazed European travellers to the city. Before the end of the century the animals were moved elsewhere and the palace served for a while as a brothel. But it was soon redeemed from this misuse, for in 1719 the famous *Tekfur Saray* pottery was set up here. This pottery produced a new kind of

The interior of the Yedikule fortress, showing how it was integrated into the existing Theodosian walls in AD 1457 by Mehmet the Conqueror.

Turkish tiles, the so-called *Tekfur Saray* type, inferior to those of Iznik and beginning to show European influence. The project, however, was short-lived, and by the second half of the 18th century the palace was in full decline and eventually lost its roof and floors. During the first half of the 19th century *Tekfur Saray* served as a poorhouse for Jews and in the present century it housed a bottle works before being abandoned altogether. Today it is a mere shell.

Caernarfon Castle, built by Edward I of England in humble imitation of the walls of Constantinople.

The influence of Constantinople on medieval military architecture

Many were the rulers of western Europe who passed beneath the walls of Constantinople as they made their way towards a crusade in the Holy Land. The sight was no doubt most impressive, and made its mark upon the military architecture that these monarchs commissioned on their return. King Edward I of England is the most quoted example, and it is no coincidence that the walls and towers of 13th-century AD Caernarfon Castle bear a strong superficial resemblance to the monumental 5th-century AD wall of the Byzantine emperor Theodosius II. Edward I commanded an army on the Seventh Crusade and would without doubt have been impressed by the high curtain interspersed with polygonal, round and square towers and its banded masonry. Caernarfon Castle was intended by Edward to be symbolic of his conquest and new government of Wales, and he constructed his new hourglass-plan castle, with high curtain walls, polygonal flanking towers and great twin-towered gatehouses. Edward's symbol had to be novel, vast and majestic and derived in some way from imperial Rome, hence its Roman/Byzantine appearance. Even the masonry was made to look like the walls of Constantinople by using limestone from the Penmon quarries in Anglesey, whose tiers of courses were interleaved every so often with darker brown sandstone courses from quarries in Menai. But in reality the whole project must have been a great disappointment to him. Begun in AD 1283, it was never finished.

The walls of Constantinople today

Repairs and restoration

The walls of Constantinople were kept in constant repair throughout the Middle Ages. During the 20th century restoration took the place of repairs in a programme that was much criticised at the time. The restorations were financed in part by UNESCO, but the exigencies of the municipal authority caused the project to be rushed. The work was divided among 11 contractors, with a 'scientific consultant' assigned to each, when one could be located. In most areas the walls were over-restored and refaced rather than being repaired. Perhaps they now give a clearer idea of how the elaborate defensive system once worked, but all sorts of historical evidence may have been destroyed in the process. There does not appear to be any coordination between teams, or a plan for the publication of the results. With the change of government in 1994 the work was abruptly halted.

The programme's inadequacies, however, only became really apparent on 17 August 1999, when an earthquake of a magnitude of 7.4 on the Richter scale caused some damage to the walls. Several towers were damaged, five of them seriously. There was less effect on the southern part of the walls, although one octagonal tower lost its southern half. Several rectangular towers were damaged near the Belgrade Gate, and part of the wall fell by the Topkapi Gate. Two towers that had been restored in the 1970s and a segment of wall near the Edirne Gate also suffered. One interesting observation that was made after the earthquake was that, in many areas, the cosmetic additions of recent restorations simply fell away from the historic fabric, almost as if the walls were showing contempt for the shoddy work that had been done on them! Professor Zeynep Ahunbay, chair of Historic Preservation at Istanbul Technical University, is quoted as saying:

> The restoration campaign of the 1980s has been criticised due to its resort to the reconstruction of ruined towers and gates instead of stabilising and consolidating the dangerous structures. The behaviour of 20th-century repairs during the recent earthquake … constitutes a good lesson for future restorations.

The main section of the walls of Blachernae, showing the wall of Leo and the Prison of Anemas.

Visiting the walls

The entire length of the walls of Constantinople is readily and freely accessible to any visitor to modern Istanbul, yet few people exercise the option, which is a great pity. The walls receive cursory mention in most guidebooks, and no tour operator in Istanbul appears to offer a visit as part of their wares. There are several reasons for this. First, the major parts of the lengths of the walls are nowhere near the other main tourist sights of Istanbul. The Yedikule fortress, which incorporates the Golden Gate, is the one exception. Second, they are difficult to get to by public transport except for the Topkapi Gate area, which can be reached by the modern tramway from Eminonu. Unfortunately this is one of the least attractive parts of the wall in either direction. To the south of the Topkapi Gate the successive underpasses of the motorway render the area adjacent to the wall remote, lonely and somewhat threatening. To the north lies the *mesoteichion* section, where the siege damage is most extensive and there is probably less to see than anywhere else. It also involves a walk beside the motorway. The third consideration militating against a visit is security. In spite of the attentions of the Istanbul government long stretches of the wall do not appear to provide personal safety. In some places they provide locations for itinerants, and no tourist would wish to venture near. In other places the walls pass through very unpleasant looking areas of the city, where a visitor is regarded with suspicion. This unfortunately includes some of the best-restored sections of the wall.

The prospect of walking the entire length of the walls is therefore one that should not be undertaken lightly. However, it is possible to make select visits that should be sufficient to provide a flavour of the whole. For example, picnicking families frequent the area immediately adjacent to the Sea of Marmora on summer weekends. Here is the Marble Tower and the Gate of Christ, and although the walls end at the railway line it is perfectly possible to examine and enjoy this short stretch. Beyond the railway line lies the Yedikule fortress, which is open to the public and well worth visiting for its own sake. As noted earlier, it incorporates the Golden Gate. From the Golden Gate the walls may be climbed, and one can walk along and around them for some considerable distance. A short walk along the walls to the north from the Golden Gate is very rewarding. Here the moat area is occupied by gardens growing vegetables, and there are several fine restored sections of wall. It also appears to be the safest area. There is a main road here, not a motorway. The visitor can easily examine the walls from all directions, and enjoy various

A restored section of the outer wall near the Belgrade Gate, showing the outer walkway, towers and a gateway.

In this section just south of the Topkapi Gate we see good examples of the towers of the outer wall. One is semicircular, the other square. Both are very small compared with the towers of the inner wall behind them. The photograph was taken in 1996, since when this area has been landscaped.

A severely damaged section of wall south of the Topkapi Gate showing the outer walkway and the remains of the moat filled with sheep!

shaped towers, interesting restored sections and some fine battle-damaged towers and walls. The area becomes less pleasant as one approaches the Topkapi Gate, and the devastation (arising form the AD 1453 siege) of the *mesoteichion* section is quite striking. Unfortunately there is a motorway on one side of the walls and squalor on the other. The views get better beyond the Edirne Gate. The area of the Palace of the Porphyrogenitus, where the Theodosian walls end, is very interesting, and one may round off one's walk by making a rewarding visit to the recently landscaped area in the furthest northern point that incorporates the Blachernae Palace. It is easy to walk to the gate where the last emperor was seen alive for the last time in AD 1453, and to enjoy the new garden laid out in front of the corner of the wall.

The best view of the sea walls on the shore of the Sea of Marmara may be obtained below the Topkapi Palace. The distant view can only be seen from a ferry or a cruise ship. This sight of Constantinople, with its graceful towers and dramatic overall position, is one that has enchanted visitors for centuries, and sums up for anyone the reasons why such a precious jewel had to be defended by the finest walls in the world.

Bibliography and further reading

The literature available on the Byzantine Empire is vast, but many valuable contributions have been made over the past few years. The translations into English of primary source materials such as the *Chronicon Paschale* are particularly useful. I include below certain key works accessible to the general reader. As for the walls themselves, little exists beyond the standard work by Van Millingen.

Geanakoplos, Deno John *Byzantium: Church Society and Civilisation seen through contemporary eyes* (Chicago: University of Chicago Press, 1984)

Haldon, John *Warfare, State and Society in the Byzantine World, 565–1204* (London: UCL Press, 1999)

Haldon, John *The Byzantine Wars* (Stroud: Tempus, 2001)

Harris, Jonathan *Byzantium and the Crusades* (London: Hambledon and London Ltd, 2002)

Hearsey, John E. N. *City of Constantine 324–1453* (London: John Murray, 1963)

Heath, Ian *Byzantine Armies 886–1118* (Men At Arms 89, Oxford: Osprey Publishing Ltd, 1979)

Kaegi, Walter *Army, Society and Religion in Byzantium* (London: Variorum Reprints, 1982)

Kaegi, Walter *Heraclius Emperor of Byzantium* (Cambridge: CUP, 2002)

Mango, Cyril *Byzantine Architecture* (London: Faber and Faber, 1978)

Mango, Cyril, and Dagron, Gilbert *Constantinople and its hinterland: Papers from the Twenty-seventh Spring Symposium of Byzantine Studies, Oxford April 1993* (Society for the Promotion of Byzantine Studies 3, Variorum 1995)

Mango, Cyril *The Oxford History of Byzantium* (Oxford: OUP, 2002)

Needham, Joseph *Science and Civilisation in China Volume 5 Chemistry and Chemical Technology Part 7: Military Technology; The Gunpowder Epic* (Cambridge: CUP, 1986)

Nicol, Donald *The Last Centuries of Byzantium 1261–1453* (Cambridge: CUP, 1993)

Nicolle, David *Romano-Byzantine Armies 4th–9th Centuries* (Men At Arms 247, Oxford: Osprey Publishing Ltd, 1992)

Norwich, John Julius *Byzantium: The Apogee* (Harmondsworth: Penguin, 1991)

Ostrogorsky, George *History of the Byzantine State* (Oxford: Blackwells, 1980)

Ousterhout, Robert *Master Builders of Byzantium* (New Jersey: Princeton University Press, 1999)

Runciman, Steven *The Fall of Constantinople* (Cambridge: CUP, 1965)

Treadgold, Warren *Byzantium and its army 284–1081* (California: Stanford University Press, 1995)

Turnbull, Stephen *The Ottoman Empire 1326–1699* (Essential History Series, Osprey Publishing Ltd: Oxford, 2003)

Turtledove, Harry *The Chronicle of Theophanes* (Philadelphia: University of Pennsylvania Press, 1982)

Van Millingen, Alexander *Byzantine Constantinople: The walls of the city and adjoining historical sites.* (London: John Murray, 1899)

Whitby, Michael, and Whitby, Mary *Chronicon Paschale 284–628 AD* (Liverpool: Liverpool University Press, 1989)

Whittow, Mark *The Making of Orthodox Byzantium 600–1025* (London: Palgrave Macmillan, 1996)

Wiliamson G. A. (trans.) *Procopius: The Secret History* (Harmondsworth: Penguin, 1966)

Index

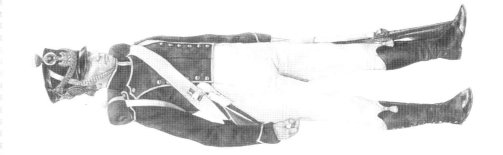

FIND OUT MORE ABOUT OSPREY

❏ Please send me the latest listing of Osprey's publications

❏ I would like to subscribe to Osprey's e-mail newsletter

Title / rank

Name

Address

City / county

Postcode / zip   state / country

e-mail

FOR

I am interested in:

❏ Ancient world   ❏ American Civil War
❏ Medieval world   ❏ World War 1
❏ 16th century   ❏ World War 2
❏ 17th century   ❏ Modern warfare
❏ 18th century   ❏ Military aviation
❏ Napoleonic   ❏ Naval warfare
❏ 19th century

Please send to:

USA & Canada:
Osprey Direct USA, c/o MBI Publishing, P.O. Box 1,
729 Prospect Avenue, Osceola, WI 54020

UK, Europe and rest of world:
Osprey Direct UK, P.O. Box 140, Wellingborough,
Northants, NN8 2FA, United Kingdom

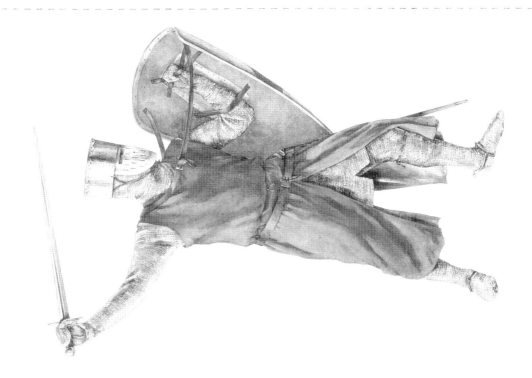

www.ospreypublishing.com

call our telephone hotline
for a free information pack

USA & Canada: 1-800-826-6600
UK, Europe and rest of world call:
+44 (0) 1933 443 863

Young Guardsman
Figure taken from *Warrior 22:
Imperial Guardsman 1799–1815*
Published by Osprey
Illustrated by Richard Hook

Knight, c.1190
Figure taken from *Warrior 1: Norman Knight 950 – 1204 AD*
Published by Osprey
Illustrated by Christa Hook

POSTCARD